Love,
Charles & Frances

7.95

HOW TO WIN YOUR CITY TO JESUS

Charles & Frances Hunter

Published by
HUNTER BOOKS
201 McClellan Road
Kingwood, Texas 77339, U.S.A.

BOOKS BY CHARLES ♥ FRANCES HUNTER

A CONFESSION A DAY KEEPS THE DEVIL AWAY
ANGELS ON ASSIGNMENT
ARE YOU TIRED?
BORN AGAIN! WHAT DO YOU MEAN?
COME ALIVE
DON'T LIMIT GOD
FOLLOW ME
GO, MAN, GO
GOD IS FABULOUS
GOD'S ANSWER TO FAT...LOØSE IT!
GOD'S CONDITIONS FOR PROSPERITY
HANDBOOK FOR HEALING
HANG LOOSE WITH JESUS
HIS POWER THROUGH YOU
HOT LINE TO HEAVEN
HOW DO YOU TREAT MY SON JESUS?
HOW TO HEAL THE SICK
HOW TO MAKE YOUR MARRIAGE EXCITING
HOW TO OVERCOME "COOL DOWN" AND KEEP THE FIRE BURNING
HOW TO RECEIVE AND MAINTAIN A HEALING
How to Receive and Minister THE BAPTISM WITH THE HOLY SPIRIT
HOW TO WIN YOUR CITY TO JESUS
I DON'T FOLLOW SIGNS AND WONDERS...THEY FOLLOW ME!
IF YOU REALLY LOVE ME...
IMPOSSIBLE MIRACLES
MEMORIZING MADE EASY
MY LOVE AFFAIR WITH CHARLES
NUGGETS OF TRUTH
POSSESSING THE MIND OF CHRIST
P.T.L.A. (Praise the Lord, Anyway!)
SINCE JESUS PASSED BY
the fabulous SKINNIE MINNIE RECIPE BOOK
STRENGTH FOR TODAY
SUPERNATURAL HORIZONS (from Glory to Glory)
THE TWO SIDES OF A COIN
THIS WAY UP!
VIDEO STUDY GUIDE - HOW TO HEAL THE SICK (14 Hours)
VIDEO STUDY GUIDE - HOW TO HEAL
THE SICK POWER PACK (6 Hours)
VIDEO STUDY GUIDE - THE BOOK OF ACTS (11 Hours)
WHY SHOULD "I" SPEAK IN TONGUES???

ISBN # 1-878209-06-X

TABLE OF CONTENTS

For information about Charles and Frances Hunter's Evangelistic Census, Harvest Celebration, and Healing Explosions, video teaching tapes, audio tapes, and books, or foreign languages for missions training, write to:

CHARLES & FRANCES HUNTER
201 McClellan Road
Kingwood, Texas 77339, U.S.A.
(713) 358-7575 or 1-800-231-3024

Foreword

GOD SAID. . ."TAKE A CENSUS OF THE WORLD!"

Not since the resurrection of Jesus have there been such shock waves ringing through hell as there have been since God said, "Take a census of the world!"

Can you visualize 20 to 30 million Christians starting at a given signal to evangelize the United States and finishing the census in two weeks?

Is it possible?

"Who has heard or seen anything as strange as this? For in one day, suddenly, a nation, Israel, shall be born, even before the birth pains come. In a moment, just as Israel's anguish starts, the baby is born, the nation begins. Shall I bring to the point of birth and then not deliver? Asks the Lord your God. No. Never!" (Isaiah 66:7,8 TLB).

WHEN WILL JESUS RETURN?

There is a stirring in the spirits of almost all believers that this is the decade in which Jesus will return! If this fact has been revealed to the body of

Christ by the Holy Spirit, then how can this be done completely, systematically, methodically, and within this time frame?

Jesus said, *"Go into all the world and preach the gospel to every creature"* (Mark 16:15). In effect He was saying, "Take a census of the world!"

With all the combined efforts of all ministries on earth, more people are being born on earth than born again.

How can we bring the change that will accomplish what Jesus promised: The gospel will be preached to every person on earth and then He will return?

The fragmented, denominationalized body of Christ Jesus must come into the unity prescribed in Ephesians 4:11-16.

The only single area of the Bible in which all genuine Christian churches and people have a common agreement is the preaching of the gospel to every creature by believers trained and equipped and supervised by the five-fold ministry.

The plan Jesus made is that this would be done by *all believers preaching the gospel with signs following.*

God has always reached His people by using mankind and registered them with census-taking, a systematic, accurate way to count every person within the census area!

Can we lay down our denominational and theological differences and creeds to do what God has spoken?

Are souls more important to us than denominations?

Can we link arms with every denomination,

every organization, every Christian television and radio network and station in the world?

We know this will have to be a supernatural job, one that is too big for us Christians to handle in the natural, but can you visualize 20 million born-again believers, starting at a given signal, possibly by satellite, to take a gospel-preaching census of the entire United States, or a greater number cover the entire world?

Can you see born-again believers going across the United States like a bunch of locusts with hundreds of thousands or even millions of people being born again in one day? Can we reach every person in a nation in two weeks?

Believers are going to be the census takers. The gospel will be presented to every person so they will have an opportunity to register for the kingdom of God in this census-like systematic contact with five billion souls on earth before the arrival of Jesus!

This is the time for it to happen!

This is the decade of the harvest.

"But when He saw the multitudes, He was moved with compassion for them, because they were weary and scattered, like sheep having no shepherd. Then He said to His disciples, 'The harvest is plentiful, but the laborers are few. Therefore pray the Lord of the harvest to send out laborers into His harvest'" (Matthew 9:36-38).

We had just held our first giant Healing Explosion in Honduras and returned from this glory when God spoke those world-encompassing words, "Take a census of the world!"

God knew that we had just witnessed the United States taking what they hoped was the most accurate census of the nation.

Can we Christians do this?

Why not?

God started census taking and nations have copied His method to systematically count every person.

Jesus spoke this plan into existence in the Bible, the Spirit of God has spoken the requirement into our minds, and God, knowing we were aware of the way it was being done in America, simplified this whole plan by saying, *"Take a census of the world!"*

It is possible that the census ordered by Caesar Augustus was the first *"all the world"* census ever taken, ushering in the beginning of the New Testament when Jesus was born.

Is it possible that this *"census of the world"* is the way God wants to wrap up this era when Jesus will return to earth?

God has said to us, and probably to every leader in the world, "What you do, do quickly!"

Jesus said that to Judas in order to finalize the Old Testament and start the New Testament; now He is saying the same to us to finalize the works of the New Testament in preparation for *His arrival!* Hallelujah!

All of us must move rapidly into this final day of harvest, and we solicit your call or letter to let us know your desires, vision, willingness to do this census-like world witness.

We need to know who God wants to use to organize this "Thrusting in of the sickle" so the earth will be reaped — this decade.

The body of Christ is scattered and shattered

into a multitude of denominations.

Now is the time to come together as a unified army — one single army to wrap up this age.

This is history in the making!

As you *"study"* this book, please do not think of how we have done things in the past, but look at this "NOW" thing God is doing on earth. By the time you read this book, the evangelization census will have been completed in Honduras.

Other nations are being planned, and cities in the United States and other nations are commencing their census-type evangelization.

Names such as Venezuela, Costa Rica, Guatemala, El Salvador, Mexico, Cuba, Japan, Chicago, Florida, Phoenix, Tulsa, Anchorage, Washington, D.C. are looming up as being ready to see the gospel preached by a unified army of believers to do the one thing for which Jesus came to earth . . . *"to save the lost!"*

Is one soul or a billion or more souls worth it before Jesus returns?

Can we do this in the United States?

Can we take nations for Jesus in two weeks?

"Shall I bring to the point of birth and then not deliver? asks the Lord your God. NO. Never!" (Isaiah 66:8 TLB).

YES WE CAN!

Chapter 1
The Heartbeat of God!

What is God saying to the body of Christ today?

At a recent national meeting they asked several of us what we thought God was saying in the twentieth century.

Someone said, "He's saying, 'Let's get more serious with prayer!'"

And that's a good thing!

Another said, "We ought to all become involved in fighting abortion!"

And that's a good thing!

Another said, "We ought to take a stronger stand against pornography because of our young people!"

. . .And that's a good thing!

A man said, "God is saying that we're going to experience more power in this next decade than ever before!"

On and on went the ideas until they got to us!

What IS God saying to the body of Christ today? Is He saying to have marriage seminars?

. . .And that's a good thing!

Is He saying to have youth programs?

. . .And they are a good project!

Is He saying to have Spiritual Warfare Conferences?

. . .And that's a good thing!

Is He saying to have Church Growth Conferences?

. . .And that's a good thing!

Is He saying to have praise symposiums?

. . .And they're a good thing, too!

Is He saying to have this? And is He saying to have that?

No, God is saying the same thing He said two thousand years ago through His son, Jesus, and He hasn't changed His mind!

"Go into all the world and preach the gospel to every creature. He who believes and is baptized will be saved, but he who does not believe will be condemned, and these signs will follow those who believe!

In My Name they will cast out demons;

In My Name *they will speak with new tongues;*

They will pick up serpents; and if they drink anything deadly, it will by no means hurt them;

They will lay hands on the sick, and they will recover!" (Mark 16:15-18).

What a wonderful thing it would be if we all had a heart that beats exactly like God's!

His heartbeat is souls, souls, souls!

An amazing thing happens to people when they get the very heartbeat of God.

It's amazing what happens when you lead somebody to Jesus; it's also amazing when you don't.

Here is a heartbreaking story that took place many, many years ago — before the tragedy of the bombing of Pearl Harbor.

Two young Japanese men came to the United States to study.

One of them went to Harvard University, the other one went to the University of Oregon.

At that time, the Asian people weren't very popular, nor were they very well accepted by the people of the United States. This was unfortunate, because I don't care who you are, or where you are, all of us have a need and a want to be loved.

We all have a need to feel that somebody wants us, that somebody likes us.

The young man who went to Harvard had so much fun made of him because he was Japanese, that he went home.

The other young man who went to the University of Oregon, also received the same treatment.

They made fun of him because he didn't look like we do. He didn't have the same color that we do, and his facial features were different than ours.

And so he, too, went home.

He later became the Prime Minister of Japan.

The first one was the man who engineered the devastating bombing of Pearl Harbor. He flew the first plane which dropped the first bomb on Pearl Harbor.

I am showing you what happened to two young men whom nobody loved enough to talk to them about Jesus.

What if somebody had talked to that young man who engineered Pearl Harbor?

Do you realize it could have changed the destiny of the world?

If somebody had only said, "God loves you, and I love you, and God has a wonderful plan for your life!"

He went back to Japan, disgruntled, unhappy and hating Americans!

Look what happened as a result!

The very heartbeat of God is souls.

Every time the heart of God beats, whether it beats like your heart beats or it beats like my heart beats, that cry is for souls, souls, souls!

God had such a passion for the lost world, that He sent His only Son to die for one reason: That you and I might be saved. He sent Jesus here to seek and to save the lost.

Each one of us needs to get the very heartbeat of God for souls!

The heartbeat of God can be a good sound or it can be a bad sound, depending on what you are doing at that particular moment.

God's heartbeat is a real steady heartbeat. It never changes its rhythm, it stays exactly the same, all the time.

I remember when I was a little girl, I didn't always do what God told me to do because I didn't know about God.

I thought God was somebody up there who had a great big spyglass in Heaven, and He was looking down at a little girl who stole a penny from her mother one time when she was four years old.

I remember when I stole that penny and bought a "sugar ball" with an almond on the inside of it that my heart went thump, thump, thump very rapidly! My heart didn't beat like God's because I was doing wrong.

But God's heartbeat kept on. His heartbeat kept on, exactly the same as it always had.

Then I went through life and my heart was not beating like God's because, like all kids, I wasn't the best little kid in the world and I did little things I wasn't supposed to do, like lie and cheat, so my little heartbeat didn't have the heartbeat of God. It just kept thumping all over the place.

I remember one day when I was eight years old and my sister was ten, we joined a church.

And for the first time in my life I felt the heartbeat of God.

I remember the Pastor didn't talk about Jesus. He just turned us around and said, "Isn't this a wonderful family? A mother and a daddy and two girls and they've joined our church," and so for a few moments my heart took on the heartbeat of God, and it felt good!

Then we left the church and the next day I went to school and I probably looked over somebody's shoulder and cheated on an exam, and so my little heart beat fast again and I am not real sure exactly the next time I heard that strong heartbeat of God, but I believe it was somewhere about the time I got married.

I remember that even though I wasn't a faithful church member, I wanted to be married in church.

I wanted to have a long white gown like everybody else and when the big day came, my heartbeat changed and during that service it was like the heartbeat of God.

It felt good!

It was wartime, and we got involved in smoking and drinking so I spent several years with a heart that forgot about God.

Then I got pregnant! Even though I wasn't a Christian, I had asked God to do me a favor.

I said to God, "I would like to have a little boy that looks exactly like his daddy! A brown-eyed boy that looks just like his father."

Once again I heard the heartbeat of God.

I remember they showed him to me and when I looked at him, I said (notice how religious I was), "My cup runneth over."

And for a little while, my heart beat like God's, because a precious life had been entrusted to me.

But then it wasn't very long before my heart was back in the world. I was smoking and drinking my martinis and not having time for God, not worrying about God!

Then my husband got critically ill.

One day the doctors told me he wasn't going to live very much longer.

Shortly after that he died!

Again I heard that strong heartbeat of God.

And I got real religious.

I thought, "God wants me to be a missionary."

My little boy was five years old at the time and I remember thinking I would have to put him in a military school.

I knew I would have to go to Africa, carry a big 78-pound black Bible and put on a long black dress, take off all my makeup, and then I would be a missionary.

Somewhere during that time period my heart began beating just a little bit like God's.

Then I looked at my little five-year-old and I

thought "No, I can't do that to him! I know what I will do instead. I'll give enough money to the church so they can add a new Sunday School room in honor of my dead husband."

Then I went back to drinking and smoking, but in the meantime God's heart kept beating.

His heart was saying, "Souls, souls, souls, souls, souls."

But my heart was too interested in having fun.

I had to work hard because I had to make a living to raise my children, so I just kept on drinking and smoking, and carrying on, but all the while God's heart kept beating.

Then one day I was in a very minor little automobile accident!

A car hit me from behind and I went up and hit my head on the windshield!

The other car spun around and hit me the second time, and this time my head went up against the side window of the car!

One of the two blows loosened the lens of my left eye and in three months that eye was totally blind!

All this time my heart was wildly beating, but God's heart beat very regularly and deliberately!

God looked down at me and knew what He was going to do!

God knew He was going to take a tragedy and make a miracle out of it.

They told me I would have to have an eye operation. . .God's heart was regularly beating all the time!

They said, "We will take your eye out, lay it on your cheek, cut off the growth that has formed as a result of this traumatic blow, we will put it back in, then, *if* you are 'lucky' we'll fit you with contacts and glasses and you may be able to have pretty good vision." (This operation is much easier now.)

My heart momentarily panicked!

I didn't like what they said to me, but it didn't really scare me because God makes us what we are in the beginning.

God gives us what He wants us to have in the beginning; we just don't use it for the purpose He intended.

I can see God looking down that day. His heart was beating for my soul, and He said, "I'm going to get her, I'm going to get her this time."

I was scheduled to be in the hospital at 5:00 o'clock that afternoon but I had a God-shaped vacuum in my heart.

Ecclesiastes 3:11 says, "*God has placed eternity into the heart of man,*" and until you fill your heart with the things of God, *nothing else* will ever satisfy.

At 4:00 I really got scared!

I didn't know God, so I didn't know to go to God!

I didn't hear that strong heartbeat of God, so I turned and looked for a bottle of gin instead.

For the next three hours I drank as many martinis as I could and by the time I got to the hospital, I was "crocked to the gills."

But when I got to the hospital, I got religion!

Everybody gets religion when they get to a hospital!

I got religion, too, so I thought I would read my Bible.

I was horrified when I discovered it was not in my suitcase.

I called up a girl friend of mine who was drunk right along with me and said, "Daria, (now watch this spirit of religion) you know I am going to be operated on tomorrow" (she had taken me to the hospital and had gotten drunk with me). "And you know I can't go to surgery without reading my precious Bible."

Then I said, "Would you go to my house and get it?"

She said, "Where is it?"

I said, "It is in the back bedroom, in the back closet, way up high on the back shelf in the back."

I said, "I haven't read it for five years, so would you please dust it off real good and bring it up to me?"

It had to be dusted off because the only time I ever read my Bible was when I went to surgery.

She went over to my house, got my Bible, dusted it off real good since I hadn't read it since I had my gall bladder taken out five years before, and then she brought it to the hospital.

I called all the nurses in because I wanted to show them what a great religious saint they had on their hands!

The heart of God was still beating rhythmically but mine had too much gin so it was racing. Nevertheless God's heart was still beating at the same rate.

I opened my Bible very dramatically and read one verse of the twenty-third Psalm, "*The Lord is my Shepherd, I shall not want.*"

Maybe during the time when I read that, my

heart, just for a moment, began to beat just like God's, but it didn't last long because I didn't know God and I didn't know Jesus.

I closed my Bible after the one verse because when I had my gall bladder taken out, it was a five-hour operation and I had read all six verses.

They told me my eye operation would only take thirty minutes so I figured that all I had to read was just one verse, so that's why I closed the Bible!

Then I thought, "I think I'll give God a break and I will pray."

Once again my martini heart was beginning to beat a little like God's, because I thought I had to pray, so I looked up and I didn't even know how to pray!

Did you know you can say the Lord's prayer ten thousand times and still not know how to pray???

I had said it that many times but I *never learned* how to pray!

I looked up and I thought, "I think I will tell God exactly the way I want it done tomorrow," so I said, "God, don't let it hurt during the operation."

Then I thought, maybe I am a little too strict on God, so I said, "You can let it hurt a little bit after the operation, but not during the operation. Thank you very much."

With that I laid back on my pillow and I could just see what a great saint I was!

I could see this blue halo light around my head going out under the doors, into all the hospital rooms and everyone in the hospital was so impressed with this great saint they had there.

Suddenly, a thought entered my mind!

"What was on that page? I quoted that from

memory! I didn't read that, I said that from memory."

I opened my Bible up to where the twenty-third Psalm had been and God had done a miracle!!!

This is why I have no difficulty believing in the supernatural!!!

God had wiped off all the printing from those pages of my Bible!

I was a printer.

I owned a printing company, and God speaks to us in a way we can understand!

He had supernaturally wiped all the printing off.

Anybody in the printing business knows once the ink is laid down, you cannot get it off!

And there it was!

Those pages in my Bible were as white as snow!!!

Suddenly I saw the finger of God!

Don't ask me how a drunken sinner knows the finger of God.

I can only tell you that I did.

It was dipped in the crimson red blood of Jesus.

I saw His finger begin to write on the pages of my Bible.

On the left hand side in the blood of Jesus He wrote, "Frances Gardner" (that was my name then) and on the right hand side in the blood of Jesus He wrote, "I love you."

I heard the heartbeat of God.

I looked up to God, (now remember I was a wild sinner, smoking five packages of cigarettes a day, drinking martinis like they were going out of style, the life of every cocktail party because I knew more dirty jokes than anybody else, couldn't open my mouth and say four words unless one was a swear word)—and as I looked up to God I said the secret of the Christian life!

I said, "God, give me back my prayer, and I promise You this. I will spend the rest of my life seeing what I can do for You, and not what You can do for me."

Beloved, that is the secret!!! Not what God can do for you, but what *you* can do for God.

Suddenly my heart began to beat a little different beat than it had ever beat before.

At that moment, a pastor came in.

He had invited me to church for four-and-a-half years.

He had prayed for me for four-and-a-half years.

I always had an excuse.

But when he came in this time I didn't even wait for him to say one word!

I said, "The first place I'm going is to your church when I get out of this hospital!"

He almost laughed out loud, because there are more promises made on a hospital bed than anyplace else. And there are more promises broken when you walk out of the hospital door than anyplace else!

However, the first place I went was to his church.

Now I am not going to tell you the whole story of how I got saved, but I want to tell you when it actually happened.

I went to church every Sunday for nine months listening to this pastor preach.

Every Sunday morning when he made the altar call he would say, "All have sinned and come short of the glory of God."

And I would say, "Not me!"

I'd say, "God, remember the tuna fish sandwiches I made? Remember all the cream cheese sandwiches I made for the women's society? Remember all the dishes that I washed? (That was in the days before dishwashers.)"

I thought I was working my way to heaven!

I knew I couldn't be a sinner, because I thought that to be a sinner you had to have murdered somebody or done some horrible thing like robbing a bank!

Suddenly there came in my heart a hunger for God!

There was that heartbeat of God.

One Sunday morning I got up and said, "God, I'm not going to leave that church until I know that I know that I know that I know, that Jesus Christ is living in my heart!

"I am not going to leave that church until I know that I know that I know that I know that I am saved!"

What a way to go to church!!! What a way to go to church!

I didn't hear a word the pastor said that morning!

That shows you that sermons aren't the only important things, because it is what your heart wants to hear that is important! I didn't hear a thing he said.

I couldn't wait for him to get to that song they had sung every Sunday for nine months, "Just as I am, without one plea, But that thy blood was shed for me."

And they didn't sing it that Sundav.

They sang, "Have Thine Own Way."

I hadn't listened to a word that was said — all I wanted was the first sound of "Just as I Am" and I knew I was going to go to the altar.

They didn't sing it!

I felt I had been betrayed.

I felt like somebody had stuck a dagger in me.

I was still standing there telling God that I was not a sinner but that I wanted to be saved.

God said, "Remember that penny you stole from your mother when you were four years old?"

My heart went thump, thump, very loud and fast!!!

Of course I remembered that penny, but I didn't think God knew about it! And if He did, I didn't think He would have remembered it that long because now I was forty-nine years of age, that was forty-five years ago!

I didn't know God would remember all that, but He did!

Then He reminded me of another sin that wasn't quite as nice. I said, "God, you knew about that one too???"

Then God said the words that changed my life. He said, "I know everything that you have ever done."

That really wasn't a shock to me because I had always heard that God had eyes, so I knew He could see.

He said, "I know every rotten, stinking thing you have ever said."

That didn't surprise me either because if God can hear prayers, He can hear anything you say, so I knew He had ears!

The third thing He said was the thing that "got" me.

He said, "I know every rotten, stinking thought you have ever had."

And then I knew God knew that I was a sinner and I cried out, "God have mercy on me, a sinner!"

Then very quickly I said, "God I'll make a deal with you."

My heart was crying so much for God that I was willing to make a deal that in the natural would not have made sense to me a short time before.

I said, "I'll give you all of me, (that was all my cigarettes, that was all of my gin, that was all of my dirty jokes) I'll give them all to you God. All of my dirty cuss words, I'll give them all to you, *in exchange for all of You.*"

My heart took on a new beat!

No longer was it rapid, erratic and fast.

That was the day that my heart started beating with the very heartbeat of God! Souls, souls, souls, souls, souls!

I looked at sin and I could not stand it!

As soon as the service was over, I rushed out to my car.

My heart was now beating like God's!

My daughter was with me and I scratched out as fast as I could!

I was saved just south of Miami, Florida, and that day I stopped at every store that was open!

I didn't know what had happened to me!

I didn't really understand salvation!

I didn't understand being born again.

All I knew was that something that so glorious, so wonderful had happened to me and I wanted to give it away; I wanted to share it with everybody!

That was Jesus living on the inside of me!

I didn't even know what to say!

As I ran into every store, I got ahold of the men and I pulled on their jackets and I said, "You have got to come to my church!"

I didn't know what else to say.

All I knew was that I thought whatever happened to me could happen to anybody in that same church.

I became a fanatic, because my heart beat for nothing but souls.

My heart beat for nothing except for people to come into the kingdom of God.

No longer was I busy thinking about myself, I was thinking about the world out there and I remembered that I was forty-nine years of age.

No one in those first forty-nine years had ever told me about Jesus!

Nobody!

I remember thinking that day, "There is nobody but me, I've got to go tell the whole world about Jesus! I have to save the whole world!"

That was exactly the way I felt.

I had to do it all by myself!

I had lived in many different cities, I had gone to many different churches, and no one had ever told me that I needed to know Jesus personally!

But when I met Him, I knew that He came to live on the inside of me.

That was the heartbeat of God!

The very first thing I did was run out and do exactly what Jesus did.

What did He talk about when He walked on earth?

The kingdom of God.

The kingdom of Heaven.

He talked to people about eternity.

That is all I wanted to talk about.

People thought I had lost my mind and I said, "I have, I now possess the mind of Christ." That was why I didn't want to talk about anything except Jesus!

I was labeled as a total fanatic.

I said, "Great."

People prophesied that I would backslide. I'd say to them, "I'll pray for you."

But do you know what I did that whole week long?

I owned a big printing company, and I looked at everybody who came into my printing company that week and thought, "They are all lost, they are dying and they are going to hell! I've got to save them all!"

I looked at every one of my martini drinking friends and I thought, "They are dying, they are lost, they are going straight to hell, and I have to save them all."

All I did that whole week long was talk about Jesus. And tell people.

I didn't even know what to say!

I didn't even know how to talk about Jesus, I just talked about something that had happened to me, and I would tell them all, "You just have to go to church with me next Sunday morning."

I was saved in a little church that was fifty years old. After fifty years, they had forty members, and they said, "We are small because we are holy."

That's a lie of the devil!

You are small because you don't open your mouth!

The next Sunday morning this wild sinner who had gotten saved with martinis on her breath and cigarette smoke all over her, had gone out and drug twenty people to the church!

Twenty of the biggest messes you ever saw in your life.

Alcoholics, drug addicts, a homosexual, a prostitute; you name it, I drug them all in.

I remember one man was so drunk, he kept falling off the pew and I'd get down, help him up and put him back on the pew again!

Finally, I gave up, and thought to myself, "Let him lay on the floor. He can hear what I heard as well on the floor as he can hear it sitting up in the chair, so I just let him lay on the floor."

All these good saints in the church said, "Tsk, tsk, tsk. Isn't that terrible, bringing people like that to church!"

Where do people like that belong?

Inside your church!!

And they will, when you have a heartbeat for God!

They prophesied over me that I'd backslide and said I'd get over it!

But the next Sunday I came in with twenty more.

Now I had forty!

After fifty years they had forty.

Now I have forty on one side, the wildest, drunkest sinners you ever saw in your life!

I'm amazed they didn't get their cigarettes out in church!

I'm amazed they didn't get their whiskey bottles out of their pockets in church, but they didn't; they just sat there and fell off the pew and talked when you are not supposed to talk!

But something had happened to me!

I got the heartbeat of God!

Suddenly, I didn't want anybody to go to hell.

Even my enemies.

I didn't want them to go to hell!

On Tuesday I was running through my big printing company and my heart was going *bang, bang, bang, bang!*

I was running so fast from one machine to another because we had a lot of work to do when suddenly I stopped right in the middle of everything.

I looked down and I could see my heart beating. I said, "That's not my heart, that's the heartbeat of Jesus living on the inside of me!"

This has to be a revelation from God. This is not something you ever learn in the natural.

I knew that I knew that I knew that I knew even though I was only two days old, a baby Christian, I knew it was Jesus living in there!

I stopped right in front of my wild, sinning employee staff and said, "Oh, Jesus, you are in there!"

I put my hand over my heart.

I said, "I shut the door! I lock it! I throw the key away! Now I've got You in there and You can't ever get out!"

My heart kept beating like the heartbeat of God! People said "She'll get over it!"

This is twenty-five years later, and my heart is still beating exactly the same way!

Give me a sinner and I won't let him go.

Not until I get him saved. Hallelujah!

I believe I am a normal Christian. I don't believe I am the abnormal Christian.

Most Christians believe that Jesus is coming soon!

Most believe that you and I are going to see the return of Jesus!

Many believe that it is sooner than we really think!

Charles and I can see the tempo of everything stepping up so rapidly.

We can see people hungering in their hearts for the things of God like they have never hungered in their entire life.

Don't pray for revival — jump into it because revival is here!

If it's not here for you, it's passing you by, because revival is here!

I believe God has placed within the heart of mankind a hunger for the things of God.

No one can ever be satisfied until he fills this God-shaped vacuum with the things of an eternal God.

Everywhere I go people are hungry for Jesus.

It doesn't make any difference what place you go to, it doesn't make any difference what country you go to, what city you go to, people are hungry for God.

In a world that thinks it is so unhappy and

thinks it is so dissatisfied, all that is wrong with them is that they are looking for God.

Don't criticize them because of what they are doing.

Give them the answer.

There is an answer and it is five letters:

J-E-S-U-S!

I didn't even know I was lost.

I didn't know I was a sinner.

I've heard people say that everybody knows they are a sinner.

Not me!

I had no idea I was a sinner because I was a good mother, I was trying to raise my children right.

I knew I wasn't a sinner!

I believe the world is full of people just like me, involved in churchianity, which is what I was involved in and yet who don't really understand what God wants for them!

I started sharing with my own family.

The second person who ever received Jesus in my ministry was my own daughter, Joan, who accepted Him thirty days after I did.

I asked her one time, "Honey, what was the one thing that made you accept Jesus so quickly after Mother did?"

She said, "Because of the *change* I saw in you — *because of the change I saw in you!*"

For years she had a drinking momma!

She had a momma who told dirty jokes!

She had a smoking momma and I don't think she ever saw her momma without a cigarette in her mouth for the first thirteen years of her life!

Suddenly, there was a momma who didn't

smoke anymore because I believe what the Bible says, "*If any man be in Christ, he is a new creature; the old things are passed away. Behold beloved, all things are become new.*" When you are a new creature in Christ, if you are sincerely and honestly born again, you have no right, you should have no desire, you should have nothing to do with your old life.

All of those things are gone!

A man came up to me recently and asked me to pray for his temper.

He said, "I'm just like my father."

I said, "Great!!!" He said, "My father has a vicious temper."

I said, "Great! Are you born again?"

He said, "Yes!"

I said, "Then you are just like God. You are not like your natural father. You have no right to those old qualities. None whatsoever. But you have a responsibility, and that is to get the heartbeat of God so there will come into your heart a hunger for the soul of every person you meet! Not a continuation of the same old sins you once had."

I often say Jesus opened my mouth and I haven't shut it since!

That is twenty-five years that I have been doing nothing except talk about Jesus.

I don't talk about anything except Jesus because I don't think anything else is worthwhile talking about.

I have eight grandchildren and two great-grandchildren, but I don't talk about them because I believe Jesus is far more important; as much as I love them and as darling as they all are, I believe it is far more important to talk about Jesus.

I have heard a lot of people say, "God never called me to be a soulwinner."

That's a lie of the devil.

God calls everyone to be a soulwinner!

The book of Matthew and Mark are two of my favorites and contain two of my favorite portions of scripture.

In the twenty-eighth chapter of Matthew, the Great Commission of the Bible appears for the first time.

When you were saved, you automatically became a part of the greatest Evangelistic Army of the world.

You have no choice. No choice whatsoever if you are saved!

In Matthew 28:18 Jesus first of all established Who He was! He said, "*All authority has been given to me in heaven and on earth.*" ALL of it.

Then in Luke 10:19 He said, "*Behold, I give YOU authority.*" Who did He give His authority to? To us believers!

"*I give YOU the authority to trample on serpents and scorpions, and over ALL the power of the enemy,*" A-L-L the power of the enemy "*and nothing shall by any means hurt you!*" First it was given to Me, now I have given it to you.

In Matthew 28:19 He said, "*Go!!!*"

If Jesus never said another word, that would have been enough!

Jesus did not call us to come and sit in wonderful padded pews.

I think they are great, I appreciate them far more than hard seats, but Jesus never called us to sit on a soft pew and do nothing else.

He said, *"Go!!"* Whether you go to the Chinese restaurant, McDonald's, Arby's, the Village Inn, Burger King, Red Lobster, Seafood Shanty, Pizza Hut, or any other place where you eat, you should never go into them unless all of those places know that Jesus is in your town.

When you go out for lunch, dinner or shopping I don't want you to talk about seafood, I don't want you to talk about pizza, I don't want you to talk about how fat or skinny you are or how hungry you are; I want you to talk about *Jesus, Jesus, Jesus.* I want you to get that heartbeat in you that will make you cry out for the souls in your area.

Jesus said, *"Go!!!"*

He didn't say *sit!*

He didn't say take three years to learn how to be a witness.

If Jesus is really living on the inside of you, if you believe *"Christ in you, the hope of glory,"* that same heartbeat that beats in the heart of God and that beats in the heart of Jesus is going to beat in you!

I remember the first time T.L. and Daisy Osborn ever stayed at our home.

I told them the first thing that I ever remember learning, and it had to be revelation knowledge, was that I knew that I knew that I knew that Jesus was living in me, *I knew it.*

There was no doubt whatsoever!

They were amazed that I immediately knew Jesus lived inside of me.

They said when they first started preaching that, they were considered heretics.

How did I know this?

Because when I prayed that prayer "Jesus, come into my heart" I meant it!

If you ask, you are going to receive!

I knew He was in there.

I knew without a doubt that Jesus was living on the inside of me!

I also knew therefore that because Jesus lived on the inside of me, I was going to walk like Jesus; I was going to talk like Jesus; I was going to act like Jesus; I was going to do exactly the same things that Jesus did!

I no longer had a right to live the kind of life that I once lived!

I had never read the Bible.

But what did I do when I got saved?

I wasn't even saved fifteen minutes before the church service was over and I immediately went up and down U.S. Highway Number 1.

I even stopped at the funeral parlor, not that I thought I could raise the dead, but I wanted to talk to the funeral director because I wanted something good to happen to him!

Jesus said, "*Go therefore and make disciples of all the nations.*"

He didn't say go and make Christians and bring them to church and have them sit down!

He said, "*Make disciples!*"

What's a disciple?

Somebody who does exactly the same thing you do.

Somebody who goes out and tells everybody about Jesus.

A pastor should never have to have an altar call in church, because believers ought to be winning them to Jesus, then bringing them to church to be matured!

I read something recently that I thought was extremely interesting!

I have never been to a Jehovah's Witness meeting.

But I discovered what they do during their church services! Do they preach a sermon? No!

They teach you how to go out and be a witness. That is exactly why cults such as these are growing faster than most churches.

What do the Mormons do?

They make you go, I mean they *make* you go door to door to door to door, knocking on doors.

Why are those two cults the fastest growing religions in America?

Because their people are out knocking on doors.

Most of the Christians I know today are just hopping from one convention to another convention. "I got so blessed over at this convention, and I got so blessed over at that convention, and I am so exhausted, but I am still going over to this convention because they have such good speakers there."

Jesus never said go hop from one convention to another, did He?

What did He say?

He said, "*Go therefore and make disciples of all the nations, baptizing them in the name of the Father and of the Son and of the Holy Spirit, teaching them to observe all things I have commanded you; and lo, I am with you always, even to the end of the age.*"

You don't just get a ticket to heaven! You have

a responsibility, you have a great responsibility, and that responsibility is to preach the gospel to every person you meet.

You might say, "Well, I don't like to do that, I like to go to church and sit!"

Listen to the beat of your heart and see what it says.

In the sixteenth chapter of Mark (he was a little wordier than in Matthew), he starts off the same way. I love that word *go!* He said, Go, man, go!! *"Go into all the world and preach the gospel to every creature. He who believes and is baptized will be saved; but he who does not believe will be condemned."*

And then He made a promise!

Can God lie???

Can Jesus lie???

Then He made a promise that He *has* to keep because He promised to keep it. A promise is a promise is a promise!

Jesus said, *"And these signs will follow those who believe.*

"In My name." What is the name? *Jesus!*

The world, the body of Christ, the church is waking up to the power that is in the name of Jesus.

They are waking up to the authority that they have in the name of Jesus.

People are fed up with dead religion!

They are fed up with dead churches.

They are fed up with a dead gospel.

The body of Christ is coming alive to a living Jesus, to a gospel that is loaded with power and signs and wonders and miracles which are following believers.

Jesus said, *"In My name they will cast out demons."*

He didn't make any exceptions whatsoever.

He said as long as you are a believer, you are going to do what I tell you to do. So He said, *"In My name you will cast out demons."*

The name of Jesus is above the name of every devil.

There is no devil that can stand in the presence of the name of Jesus.

There is no devil that can stand up against that name because the name of Jesus is above the name of cancer!

The name of Jesus is above the name of multiple sclerosis!

The name of Jesus is above the name of lupus, above scleroderma!

He said they will cast out devils.

He said every single, solitary believer will cast out devils.

People used to argue and say demons don't exist in the world today, and if you are a Christian, you can't have a demon.

You can't have demons in your soul if you are born again, but they can attack your mind or body.

Let's quit arguing about doctrinal things and let's just cast out devils.

Let's quit all this arguing and do what Jesus said. He said, *"In My name they will cast out demons."* Glory to God!!

Then He said, *"They will speak with new tongues,"* the baptism with the Holy Spirit.

Never since we got the baptism with the Holy Spirit in 1971 have we seen such a hunger, such a revival for the power of God as we are seeing today.

The Methodists are hungry!

The Baptists are hungry!

The Catholics are hungry!

The Assemblies of God are hungry!

The Word Faith churches are hungry!

The Episcopalians — there is not a denomination in which their members are not hungry for the power of God, because people are fed up; absolutely, totally, and completely fed up with dead religion and they want to see a religion that has power!

We have a religion that has power!

Power to do the things Jesus did while He was on this earth.

He said, "*They* (the believers) *will speak with new tongues,*" the baptism with the Holy Ghost.

I was saved in a non-Pentecostal church, and our church believed that speaking in tongues was of the devil, and so any time I got close to somebody who spoke in tongues, I ran as fast as I could!

They scared me silly because they said all those wicked people were of the devil!

Who is the one who says it is of the devil??

The devil himself . . . because he wants to scare off every Christian.

He doesn't *want* them to have the power of God.

We ministered at the Indianapolis 1990 Convention.

You should have seen the Catholics flock for the baptism with the Holy Ghost!!

I don't care who you are, the world is hungry for the power of God!

They want to see Jesus living on this earth the

same way He did 2,000 years ago.

He said, *"They will speak with new tongues."*

At one of our meetings in Honduras we were standing in a rain storm, the likes of which I have never seen all my life!

Thunder came, lightning came, and the rains came!

We were on an outdoor stage in a soccer field.

I had a "live" mike and they were holding an umbrella over me that had a steel point!

Our son, Tom, said, "Mother, you were a Frances Hunter lightning rod!"

The water was so deep (somebody told me they were up to their knees in that water) that when you laid hands on people and they fell under the power of God they had to swim out!

But nobody went home!

Those people were there because they were hungry for the living Jesus, and they weren't going to leave until they got Him!

When we made the call for the baptism with the Holy Ghost, the stadium emptied!

I don't think there were 5% of the people left in the stands.

They all came out in this *pouring* down rain to receive the power of God in their life!

The world is hungry!

Sometimes the only Jesus they will ever see is the Jesus in you!

How will they hear about Jesus unless He uses your lips and He speaks through you and you speak the Word of God to the people, and they see a demonstration of power?

Then He said, *"They will take up serpents; and*

if they drink anything deadly, it will by no means hurt them."

The last thing Jesus ever said while He was on the earth was, *"They,"* (the believers) *"will lay hands on the sick, and they will recover."*

God has given us healing as a tool for salvation!

Let me just give you a very, very, very, good example!

We were in Japan and a Chinese man came to our service.

He can't speak English.

We can't speak Chinese.

We can't speak Japanese!

He can't speak English so we had a wonderful time.

But for some reason or another he fell in love with us.

It is an amazing thing, even if you can't understand each other in your natural language, you can sit at the dinner table and speak with other tongues.

Neither of us had any idea what the other one was saying, except we knew that we were loving each other in the Spirit!

We had a kindred Spirit, because we were all saved and baptized in the Holy Ghost.

That was two years ago.

Suddenly, they discovered he was loaded with cancer.

The doctors wanted to carve him into pieces.

They could give him no hope.

He said, *"No.* I go to the United States. I find Charles and Frances. They lay hands on me. I recover."

He flew from Tokyo, where he lives, to Los Angeles and called our office.

He discovered that we were in New Jersey.

He flew to New York City. He got off the plane and rode a train for three hours in a pouring down rain storm to come to the meeting just for us to lay hands on him.

I could hardly believe what he looked like!

He had lost so much weight; he was just skin and bones! He looked terrible! My heart went thump...thump...thump...

When you have the heartbeat of God, what do you want to do?

Heal the sick!

My heart cried when I saw him and saw what the devil had done to him, but I also believe that God honors faithfulness.

That man had gone to all that trouble to come to our meeting.

There was no doubt in my mind that God was going to heal him!

We laid hands on him, commanded that spirit of cancer to come out, commanded every cancer cell to die, in the name of Jesus.

He fell out under the power of God and someone took a picture of him and he looked like a corpse laying on the floor!

A few months later we were in California, and our little Chinese friend showed up at our meeting!

Totally healed by the power of God!!!

He had the doctors' records with him!!

We still can't talk to each other, but he had it translated into English so we could read it.

The doctors said he was a miracle of God. (They

were Spirit-filled!)

God gave us healing as a tool.

I believe he brought every Chinese person in central California to the meeting.

Why did they get saved?

Because they had seen a miracle of a living God!!!

It wasn't a dead god.

It was a living God they saw because they saw proof of a member of their own family who had cancer.

They all knew he was dying and now he is alive and well!!!

He got up in front of the church and through an interpreter he testified as to what God had done in his life.

We went from there to San Diego and all of his Chinese friends who had heard the story of what God had done to their Chinese brother were there.

God gave us healing as a tool so we could win the lost and bring them into the kingdom of God.

It's a wonderful tool that God has given us!

Some people say, "Well, God didn't call me to heal the sick." Yes, He did if you believe the Bible!

Jesus said, "Every believer will lay hands on the sick and they will recover."

If He said it, it has to be true!

It doesn't mean just a few select persons over here, and a few select persons over there, it means *every* believer.

And if you are not doing what Jesus said to do, then you are not fulfilling your role as a Christian!

We need the heartbeat of God on the inside of us so our hearts will beat with the very heartbeat of

God!

Would you like to see your whole area saved for the kingdom of God?

Would you like to see everybody in your area so turned on for Jesus that the devil would be afraid to come into your neighborhood because he would say, "I can't even sneak in there unless somebody opens their mouth about Jesus!"

Who does God use?

God uses people.

God doesn't preach the gospel.

The angels don't preach the gospel.

Jesus doesn't preach the gospel.

We do!

Christ in you, the hope of glory!

That's what it says in Col. 1:26-27. *"Christ in you, the hope of glory."*

When we can get that revelation that it is actually Jesus who lives on the inside of us, Jesus who controls our thoughts, Jesus who controls our mouth, and Jesus who controls our minds, then we are not going to do anything except what the Lord Jesus wants us to do.

We are believing that everyone who reads this book will want to have that hunger in their heart! So much so that you can't stand it when you see a sinner!

I can't stand it when I see a sinner.

I can't stand it when I see somebody who is not saved.

I have tremendous boldness.

We are going to believe that as you read this book you are going to begin to say things you never dreamed you would say in your entire life.

You are going to be so bold that you are going to go out there and you are going to get the sinning world by the neck!!!

And you are going to bring them into the kingdom of God!

Let me share a story with you showing you that everyone is hungry for God.

Charles and I were at a Healing Explosion and fortunately, or unfortunately, I don't know how you look at it, we have so little time when we can ever go shopping that we had been trying to get Charles a suit for two years and never had time to go to a store.

We got to the Healing Explosion one day early and I said, "Honey, do you think there might be a store that might have a nice-looking suit for you?"

We found one quickly and Charles was having the alterations made.

I want to show you how easy it is to lead somebody to Jesus.

You can take whatever they say and turn it around for the glory of God!

The salesman said to me, "Are you from this city?"

I said, "No, I am from Houston, Texas."

I immediately knew what his next question was.

"What are you doing here?"

I replied, "We are having a Healing Explosion at the auditorium on Sunday afternoon. You are going to see hundreds of people healed and you are going to see thousands receive the baptism in the Holy Ghost. God is really moving in a special way today and people are really hungry for the things of God!"

I said, "God has placed eternity in the heart of every man and I don't care who you are, I don't care how rich you are, I don't care how good you are, there is a hunger for God in your heart that will never be satisfied until you fill it with the things of an eternal God."

I continued, "You could try to fill this vacuum in your heart with sex, with lust, with money, with fame, with fortune, with drugs, with alcohol..."

He said, "Stop."

He said, "Why did you come in this store today?"

I said, "Why do you ask that?"

He said, "You just described me. I tried to find the answer in sex, in lust, in money, in fame, in fortune, in drugs, in alcohol, and I am miserable!"

I said, "Great, I have the answer!" I said, "Repeat this prayer after me right now."

I don't ask people if they want Jesus.

This is just the way God has allowed me to do it because He has given me an extra dose of boldness.

I said, "Repeat this prayer after me."

The reason I do that is because a sinner doesn't know he needs to be saved!

He is too dumb to know he needs to be saved!

So you have to take the initiative.

I said, "Repeat this prayer after me."

He immediately repeated the prayer, and when he repeated it he began to weep all over the place as God's Holy Spirit convicted him.

He came to the Healing Explosion on Sunday, we put him in a good church and today he is no longer looking for the answer to life.

Why?

Because somebody opened their big mouth.

When a church says to me, my church is little because of one reason or another, it's small because of one reason, and only one reason!

Your people have got their mouths shut.

The little church where I was saved had to go out and build a great big sanctuary in six months because it took one person with a big mouth to fill a church to the point where you couldn't get anybody else in or around it!

Wouldn't you love to see every church double its size because it got so many people talking about the Lord Jesus!!

The only reason a church stays little is because people don't talk about Jesus!

It only takes one person!!

One man, one woman, with a big mouth can change a city, can change a nation, can change a church!!!

What will happen when everybody in the church does what Jesus did and told us to do?

Soul winning should be a natural thing!

It should be a lifestyle!

We should automatically go down the street and look for everybody we can see who needs to know Jesus.

Every time I drive down a street and see somebody with a cigarette in their mouth, I curse it in the name of Jesus!

I say, "Father, let them vomit the next time they smoke one!"

Of course, with the air-conditioned cars they can't hear what I am saying; but I never see somebody in a car who is smoking unless I pray for their soul and I pray that they will be delivered from cigarettes!

I never see anyone going into a bar unless I ask God to do something about it.

Praying is wonderful!

We all believe in prayer!

But prayer is not enough! There has to be more than prayer!

When Charles and I were first married, there was a Bible college close to us and the kids loved to pray.

Twice a week, they would pray until 4:00 AM!

They had such a burden for the lost in their neighborhood.

There were many homosexuals over in that neighborhood.

They had such a burden for them that they prayed and they prayed and they prayed until 4:00 in the morning, two nights a week.

I said, "What else did you do?"

They looked at me like I had lost my head or something!

I said, "Did you go out and ask them if they wanted to accept Jesus?"

"No, we were too exhausted from praying!"

Don't let prayer (love me while I say it) *overshadow your feet!!!* I will say that again: *"Don't let prayer overshadow your feet!"*

The first time you hear something it becomes information, and that is all it is!

You can know the Bible from Genesis to Revelation, you can quote every word that is in that Bible and you can still not know what it means.

That is information until the Holy Spirit of

God takes it into your heart where it becomes revelation; and suddenly the Word of God literally explodes!

"Christ *in* you, the hope of glory!"

That is *me* God is talking about.

He is talking about Jesus living on the inside of me! He is talking about Jesus talking through me, just like Jesus talked to the people on earth in a body that He had when He lived down here!

That is revelation when you suddenly realize *you are* literally a walking Jesus on this earth.

Some people may disagree with you!

But. . .that is exactly what the Bible says in Col. 1:26, "*. . .Christ in you, the hope of glory.*"

It is not Jesus dragging you along.

It is not you running to an altar every Sunday, crying about your aches and your pains and your everything else!

It is Christ *in* you, which is the hope of glory.

Then to let Jesus use you as He lives in you, this information must go into your heart, and then into your feet so you will *go* and preach the gospel.

Without your feet going, you will only "sit" in church, but Jesus said, *"Go!"*

Every pastor who wants to know what God is saying should know that *God has not changed His mind!!!*

The heartbeat of God has never changed!

We have a responsibility — every pastor, every evangelist — we have a responsibility to every believer to put a hunger in their heart to be a witness for Jesus; to go out and do the things Jesus told us to do."

Someone recently placed a book by T.L. Osborn called SOULWINNING in our hands. It was an old copy, and it was yellow on the inside.

It is one of the most outstanding books we have ever read to fan the flames of your heart for soulwinning!

Here is an extract from the book:

Let's Take A Journey

How would you like to visit the early church?

Would their lifestyle of soulwinning interest you? How do you think they went about it? Who were the preachers? How many were witnesses? What denomination was the largest or the most popular?

What is your personal concept of the church in New Testament times? Could we follow its example, or have times changed too much?

Let's take a journey in our minds back to those churches. Stopping at the church at Ephesus, let's imagine a conversation we might have:

"Good evening, Aquila. We understand you're a member of the church here. Could we come in and visit for awhile?"

"Certainly. Come in."

"If you don't mind, we would like for you to tell us about the way the churches here in Asia Minor carry on their soulwinning program. We read that you have been a member of a church in Corinth and Rome, as well as this one here in

Ephesus. You should be very well qualified to tell us about evangelism in the New Testament church. If you don't mind, we'd like to visit your church while we're here."

"Sit down. You're already in the church. It meets here in my home."

"You don't have a church building?"

"What's a church building? No, I guess we don't."

"Tell me, Aquila, what is your church doing to evangelize Ephesus? What are you doing to reach the city with the gospel?"

"Oh, we've already evangelized Ephesus. Every person in the city clearly understands the gospel."

"What?"

"Yes. Is that unusual?"

"How did the church do it? You certainly don't have radio, television, or electronic communication. Did you have a lot of evangelistic campaigns?"

"No. As you have probably heard, we tried mass meetings in this area, but most of the time we would end up in jail."

"Then how?"

"We just went to every home in the city. That's the way the church in Jerusalem first evangelized that city.[1] The disciples there evangelized the entire city of Jerusalem in a very short time. All the other churches in Asia Minor have followed their example."

"Is it effective everywhere?"

"Yes, it is. There are so many converts that some of the pagan leaders fear their own religions will die. When Paul left Ephesus for the last time, he reminded us to keep on following this same procedure."[2]

"Aquila, this is amazing! At this rate, there is no telling how many people are going to hear the gospel and respond."

"Oh, haven't you heard? We've already shared the gospel with every person in Asia Minor, both Jews and Greeks."[3]

"That's not possible. You can't mean everyone!"

"Yes, everyone."

"But that would include Damascus, Ephesus, dozens of large cities, as well as towns and villages. What about the nomadic tribes on the desert? How long did it take the churches to reach all of these people?"

"Not long; 24 months to be exact.[3] The same thing is happening in North Africa and Southern Europe. The gospel has reached Spain, too. We've heard of a land called England, and several Christians may be there by now."

"Aquila, what you're telling us is incredible. You have done more in one generation than we have done in a thousand years!"

"That's strange. It's been rather simple for us to do. It's hard to realize things have moved so slowly for you. Maybe there is a better way to spread the good news."

[1]Acts 5:42 [2]Acts 20:20 [3]Acts 19:10

You and I are living in times that are different than anyone has ever had the privilege of living before. There is no question in our minds whatsoever. I'd rather be alive today than any other time in the history of the world.

I would rather be alive today because you and I are getting to see things that no other generation has ever, ever seen in their entire life.

There's one of two things we can do.

We can either jump in the middle of the stream and swim or drown.

I'm going to be in the middle of the stream.

I'm not a good swimmer at all but I'm right smack in the middle of the stream because I know God's going to keep my head above water the whole time.

You can be a piece of dry wood that lays on the shore and let's the sun bleach you out and you get drier and drier and deader and deader.

As for me and my house we choose to serve the Lord.

We choose to let our faith go out beyond our minds!

Glory to God!

Would you like to belong to a New Testament Church?

That's all there is to it, just going and knocking on every door!

Knocking on every door. *Knocking on every door.*

Talking about Jesus. *Talking about Jesus. Talking about Jesus. Talking about Jesus.*

The world behind that door is hungry.

They are hungry, they are miserable, they are unhappy.

Why are young people on drugs?

Why are they on alcohol?

Why is alcohol the biggest problem in the United States today?

Why do we have so many cases of AIDS?

Why do we have so much sin and immorality?

The world is hungry! Hungry!

They are hungry!

And the only thing that will answer that hunger in their heart is for people to get a heart like Jesus!

If that's what you want, put your hand on the top of your head. Stomp your foot. Say, "From the top of my head, to the tip of my toes, God, put in my heart the heartbeat of Jesus. Let my heart cry out for the sinner. Let me be what Jesus wants me to be. Father, give me a boldness, a holy boldness like I have never had. And Father, give me until Jesus comes back. . .

THE HEARTBEAT OF GOD!"

Chapter 2
The Decade of Harvest

God did not call us to preach a powerless gospel!

God did not call us to serve a powerless God!

God did not call us to live a powerless life!

He called us to be mighty warriors during this period of time which most people are calling either the DECADE OF HARVEST or the DECADE OF DESTINY.

Either name is suitable, but if Jesus is coming soon, and we all believe that He is, then we must do something about it!

We need to rise up as the glorious unified, holy, victorious army that we are because Jesus is coming back for a triumphant church and not a weak powerless church!

Jesus said that the gospel would be preached to every creature on earth by believers doing signs and wonders, then He would return.

As we have ministered around the world in all types of meetings and across denominational lines, we have asked the question, "How many believe that Jesus could well be back this decade?"

Almost without exception every hand quickly goes up.

Then we ask the question, "How are we going to get the gospel preached to every person on earth, all five billion of them, and still meet this deadline?"

God already knows the exact twinkling of an eye when Jesus will come back and probably by now Jesus knows that too, but He will come back at that exact time God decided at the very beginning of time.

That means that Jesus will get this job done through His people on earth right on time for His mighty glorious return!

If more people are being born physically than born again every year, then something isn't working like Jesus described it and planned it.

We began to search in the Bible for the answer to this great question.

One thing we discovered was that Jesus came to earth to be our model.

He set up a prototype plan for the salvation of all the people on the earth who will believe in Him and be saved.

Jesus came to earth for one single purpose, to bring people into the kingdom of God — to save the lost. He set up His prototype plan very, very simply and demonstrated it on earth in the first church.

First of all, He preached about the kingdom of God.

He did signs and wonders so they would believe and He told them exactly how to get saved.

He kept His disciples with Him during His three-and-a-half years of ministry and by example

He taught them how to do everything He did.

Then He said that everything He did, we believers would do also and even greater things. John 14:12 says, *"Most assuredly, I say to you, he who believes in Me, the works that I do he will do also; and greater works than these he will do, because I go to My Father."*

Please note that Jesus did not only say that we *could* do them, He said we *would* do them! Whenever we read that scripture, we always put the emphasis on the word *"Do!"* He meant that we would actually *do* them!

Then as Jesus was departing from this earth, He left some instructions with His disciples as to what He wanted accomplished before His return. Jesus said, *"Go into all the world and preach the gospel to every creature"* (Mark 16:15).

We have failed for 1990 years to accomplish the work Jesus assigned to us, so how are we going to get it completed before the return of Jesus, which everyone seems to feel is imminent.

Jesus never said go and sit down in a church, enjoy yourself, have a wonderful time during all of the services, and then when you die you'll go to heaven.

The Christian life is a life of action!

It is not a sedentary life!

It is a life where we are active all the time because Christianity is a lifestyle, a way of life, and not a religion.

The word "Go" as used in Mark 16:15 means "as you are going," preach the gospel!

Many of us think we could never make it to Africa, we could never make it to Central America, we could never make it to Asia, we could never go to India, but that word actually means "as you are going," preach the gospel to every creature. When He said to go into all the world, He didn't say that we all had to go to Africa or some foreign country, because some of the best gospel that needs to be preached is inside the walls of our own home.

If you have an unsaved spouse, the gospel should be preached in the bedroom!

If you have unsaved children, it should be preached over the breakfast table so they can hear the gospel and they can come into the kingdom of God!

We should never wait until the time comes along when we will have a great big opportunity to talk to crowds of 100,000!

So many people use their imagination to think that's where they start preaching the gospel.

No, it starts in your own home, in your own neighborhood, in the home of your friends, in the home of your relatives, "as you are going" into *your* world, preach the gospel to every creature.

This means preaching it to every person possible: the person in the grocery store, the person in the cleaners, the person at the service station, the person in the restaurant, at the park, at the ballgame, on the golf course, at the swimming pool — preach the gospel *as you are going!*

Don't miss any opportunity.

Jesus was establishing a pattern, a model for this end decade work of the body of Christ.

Go back and read it again and see that He was

laying every little foot print, every little brick in the sidewalk, every foundation for what we need to do.

If we will look back at what He did and not to the modern ways of doing things, it will work!

The modern way is losing ground even though we're getting millions born again in the world. We're losing billions because we're not doing it like Jesus said.

We are like a builder ignoring the architectural-engineering plans.

We're doing work by radio, by television, by missionaries, by evangelists, by pastors, by cell-groups — we're doing it by every means possible and every one of these are effective and good, but they're not doing it entirely like Jesus said!

If we are not making the success that Jesus said we should and we're closing out this time on God's calendar, then we must go back and rediscover the foundation and do it from there.

Jesus' plan was to take all of the believers, mature them, develop them, train them, equip them, make disciples out of them and send them out to do the work for the five-fold ministry.

We have been trying to do it from the pulpits, from the platforms, from the leadership position instead of training and equipping the believers to go out and do all that Jesus said. Jesus said to be witnesses with supernatural demonstrations.

Jesus completed His entire ministry in 3-1/2 years. He said and did everything His Father told Him to do in just that short time. The whole known world heard about Jesus and His mighty works.

Jesus turned all of His future work over to the apostles and disciples and to those of us who would follow them. In only two years the gospel was preached by this early church to all of Asia Minor (most of the then known world). What an awesome accomplishment, even with the horrible persecution they endured.

Could it be that the gospel will be preached to all of the now known world in 3-1/2 years, or two years? Does this sound impossible?

Could the starting of this time be soon if it is to be accomplished as it was in the church's beginning?

Is God saying to this racing generation, *On your mark, get set, go!*

Blow the trumpet in Zion, And sound an alarm in My holy mountain!

That was the sound of destruction to the Jewish nation, but now we all feel in our spirits that the sound of the alarm is the preparation for the final act to prepare God's people for the triumphant return of our Savior Jesus!

Is God saying to you and to us, blow the trumpet to alert the Christians of this decade that Jesus is returning, and we have a work to be completed before He arrives?

If we believe this is the last decade before Jesus returns, then we MUST ACT QUICKLY!

Belief without action is dead, just as faith without works is dead.

Every time God has spoken clear and distinct words to us, we have sprung into action immediately, and we have seen His wonderful miracles by the thousands in reply to our response.

Look at this scripture a little differently perhaps than you have before: *So then faith comes by hearing* (God), *and hearing* (God) *by the word of*

God (Romans 10:17).

Most of the miracles we have seen in our ministry have come with certainty when God has spoken them to us. So then our faith comes when we hear God, and we hear God because we meditate day and night in His word, which enables us to hear Him.

The timing of God and fulfillment of great portions of biblical prophecies is speaking loudly and clearly to the body of Christ today.

We heard a rhema word from God on March 31, 1990, when He said to the body of Christ, "Take a census of the world."

We heard this word from God distinctly, clearly, unmistakably, and loudly. That has brought to us "Faith without a doubt" for the fulfillment of this vision. We pray that this will reach the depth of your heart and you will hear this as a rhema word to you, too!

We feel that our personal responsibility is at this time, and at least, to blow the trumpet announcing to the Christians of this decade what God spoke, and to set up Honduras as the model nation to let the world know that God is changing His tactics of evangelism to accomplish a complete work so every person in Honduras, in your city, your state, your nation, and finally the world WILL HEAR THE GOSPEL before the return of Jesus.

He who has an ear, let him hear what the Spirit says to the churches (Revelation 3:6).

Chapter 3
"What You Do, Do Quickly!"

A few years ago as we were sensing in our spirits that we were in the foothills of the end times, God woke me at about 4:30 o'clock in the morning and said,

"What you do, do quickly!"

I jumped out of bed, grabbed my Bible and read in all the gospels the account of the last supper where Jesus spoke to His disciples. Then in John 13:27 were the words God had just spoken to me, *What you do, do quickly*.

Although these were for Judas to do his traitor betrayal of Jesus, I felt God was saying something else for this generation.

As I meditated on this, asking God what He was saying to us for today, I realized that Jesus was not just relating this act of Judas, but that actually this act, followed by the death and resurrection of Jesus, ended one era and started another.

The dictionary defines an era as "an event or date that marks the beginning of a new or important period in the history of something; a period of time measured from some important occurrence or date; a system of reckoning time by numbering the years from some important occurrence or given point of time; as, the Christian *Era* is dated from approximately four years after Jesus' birth".

It became clear that what really happened when Jesus said, "What you do, do quickly", was that He was finalizing the Old Testament period and starting the New Testament era.

Realizing that we are nearing Jesus' return, another era is about to end and a new time period is ready to start.

Our end-decade of reaching every creature on earth with the gospel must be a quick work.

God is saying to this decade, *What you do (church) do quickly.*

In John 9:4 Jesus said, *"I must work the works of Him who sent Me while it is day; the night is coming when no one can work."*

Now is the time when we all should be saying the same thing, "I must work the works of Him who sent me while it is day."

We need to complete the works of Jesus because the harvest is so ripe and it is so ready.

We need to all get out there quickly and reach every soul we can for Jesus, using powerful signs and wonders by hundreds of millions of believers.

But we say, "How is this going to be done?" If we have failed all these many years, what must be done to accomplish what Jesus promised would be done before He returns?

We have tried every conceivable way to make our churches bigger, to make even the kingdom of God bigger by various methods and procedures of trying to get the work done that God has assigned to us.

It's like we are all doing our own little thing in our part of the world.

There's overlapping!

There's duplication!

More serious than that, there are omissions of a major part of the people of the world.

Magazines and ministry reports are full of articles about this decade of harvest, decade of destiny, this final short time of reaching the whole world with the gospel.

Many ministries are training thousands of witness teams to saturate cities, touch multitudes in a nation, and to make vast strides toward reaching the world.

We see the effects of the Spirit of God alerting and leading ministries to accomplish this massive spreading of the gospel to all the world. Hallelujah!

God's Holy Spirit is stirring the hearts of the billions of sinners and lukewarm Christians, and now He is getting Christians ready to reap this vast harvest of souls — *quickly!*

When we realize that 1,990 years have gone by and over half the world has not heard the name of Jesus we know that we must do something mighty and quickly, but differently than ever before, in order to reach five billion people before Jesus comes back.

Jesus spoke this into existence so it cannot fail any more than when God said, "Let there be light," light could not fail and it came into being and still exists.

Jesus spoke the Great Commission into existence and said we are not going to miss one person!

The Bible even says that God desires that none would perish and that every person is going to have an opportunity by the Spirit of God to hear the gospel before Jesus comes back.

The following is an excerpt from our book SUPERNATURAL HORIZONS — from Glory to Glory written in 1983, showing how quickly God can do this final work before the return of Jesus.

THE PLOWMAN SHALL OVERTAKE THE REAPER

By Frances

"Behold, the days are coming," says the Lord,
"When the plowman shall overtake the reaper,
And the treader of grapes him who sows seed;
The mountains shall drip with sweet wine,
And all the hills shall flow with it.
I will bring back the captives of My people Israel;
They shall build the waste cities and inhabit them;
They shall plant vineyards and drink wine from them;
They shall also make gardens and eat fruit from them.
I will plant them in their land,
And no longer shall they be pulled up
From the land I have given them."
Says the Lord your God (Amos 9:13-15).

As we were describing the various and unique ways God has been dealing with us in the area of the "greater" things, Alan Jandl, who pastors the great Living Stones Church in Alvin, Texas, shared that scripture with us and the explanation given in his book SEND THE WORD!

He said that God had awakened him at 5 o'clock one morning and began to deal with him concerning the rapid increase that is going to take place according to His word.

He said, "I read that first verse over and over.

"Finally, way down inside of me, I began to see a man sowing grape seeds.

"As soon as they hit the ground, immediately a vine would grow and grapes would form, and a man would pick them, put them in a trough and tread out those grapes.

"That is a supernaturally fast rate — to plant and have God instantly add the increase."

And when is that day going to be?

The rest of the scripture tells us that it will occur when the mountains shall drip with sweet wine, and today grape vineyards cover the former wastelands of Israel.

God said that He would bring back the captives of Israel who would then rebuild their cities and inhabit them.

This is happening today in Israel.

Israel became a nation in 1944 and raised their flag in 1948 and they have been making gardens and eating fruit from them. Today Israel is raising more fruit per square foot of ground than any other nation in the world.

And God has promised that Israel shall never be pulled up again from their land.

The time for the supernaturally natural fast rate with an instant increase before the seed even goes into the ground is *right now* because all of the rest of the things which were mentioned in that scripture have been fulfilled!

Visualize in your spirit, if you can, the supernatural growth of a grape seed dropped into the ground and its maturity within the twinkling of an eye, almost before it hits the ground, and then visualize the miraculous power of God accelerating and accomplishing the same things in salvation, baptism with the Holy Spirit, healings and deliverance.

Visualize one word spoken, and salvation received!

Visualize one hand waved over the multitudes, and see them all healed by the power of a loving God . . . instantly!

Visualize instantaneous deliverance of hundreds of thousands of demon-possessed or oppressed people!

When is this going to happen? Today — right now, if we will learn that fine tuning that is necessary to be able to operate in those things which the Holy Spirit is trying to communicate to us!

This is a further excerpt from our book SUPERNATURAL HORIZONS — from Glory to Glory, further showing God's speed in the final harvest season.

IT'S BEGINNING TO RAIN

By Charles

God is moving so rapidly we can hardly keep up with Him. On Monday, September 20, 1982, I had a supernatural visitation from the Lord in the form of a vision.

IT'S BEGINNING TO RAIN!

It is 3:26 o'clock in the morning as I write this because God just gave me a vision that stirred my heart and I began to weep. God said, "Write it now!"

I saw a farmer admiring his bountiful crop of grain which was extremely beautiful. He had worked hard all year, and now, finally his work was almost complete and his grain was glistening in the sunlight as he prepared to bring in the combines the next morning to start harvesting the greatest bumper crop he had ever seen. He was so proud and happy about this field of beauty.

God said, "This is likened to the Kingdom of Heaven except that instead of Jesus saying it to the early Church, He is saying it now to the disciples of this end-time Church."

The farmer was wiping the sweat off his brow and the heat of the fall months didn't bother him at all because he saw in his farmer spirit the tons and tons of this rich grain already in the bins, and he was very pleased.

Suddenly he felt a breeze begin to blow. In what seemed only moments to him, it blew stronger and stronger, and then he saw clouds beginning to form. He was a farmer and he knew the signs of rain, and fear struck him as he realized that it was beginning to sprinkle.

He began to run toward the house to get help and saw his neighbor. He yelled with all his voice, "COME, COME HERE AND HELP ME! THE RAIN IS GOING TO RUIN MY BEAUTIFUL GRAIN AND I NEED HELP. HELP!!! HELP!!! HELP!!!

But his neighbor yelled back, "I NEED HELP, TOO! COME QUICKLY!"

The farmer saw other neighbors, but all of

them had the same problem because all the farms had billions of grains and it had to be gathered NOW or it would be too late!

It was a sudden storm, totally unexpected, and it came fiercely! It was beginning to rain harder and harder and even some sleet came down and the farmer could do nothing. It was horrible!

He stood watching, but could do absolutely nothing. He was completely helpless. The sleet was not noticeable as it pelted his face, and his tears came pouring down almost like the streams of rain, because ALL HE HAD — EVERYTHING was being destroyed in minutes right before his eyes!

Then the rains stopped, almost as suddenly as they had started, and the silence was so great that it was like the whole world had come to a sudden halt, and everything in God's creation became silent. Not a sound could be heard except the weeping of the farmer, but it was too late! TOO LATE! IT WAS GONE! IT WAS ALL GONE!

Then in my vision God said, "This is the end age in which you are living right now. You are the disciples of this generation and the work must be done quickly or it will be too late."

He reminded me of the billions of souls around the world who don't know Jesus, and showed me a flashback of the billions of grains on the stalks, ready for harvest.

He said He needed help.

He depends upon His people to do ALL the harvesting.

He has hosts of angels working, but they are sent as fellow-servants to help.

God said as a reminder of the plea of Jesus,

"The harvest truly is great, but the laborers are few; therefore pray the Lord of the harvest to send out laborers into His harvest" (Luke 10:2).

God showed this so clearly to me in the vision that my whole body shook because of the weeping when the realization was made so vivid that it's beginning to rain, Rain, RAIN, and that WE are the harvesters of this final crop.

It is a bumper crop and the people all over the world are so ready to accept Jesus, but God said even His believers are too busy looking at their bounty, even the bountiful knowledge of the Word, that they are not alert to the ready fields, and the rains are coming suddenly as a thief in the night. It will be too late unless the course is changed NOW.

God said, "Cry out to the other Christians and tell them as loudly as you can yell, 'HELP, HELP, HELP! ALL IS GOING TO BE LOST.'" Then he continued and said, "But yet there is a little time left and I will call upon my people and they will respond and I have sent great hosts of angels from heaven to aid in this final great harvest. I don't want any of them to perish!"

We are the disciples of this end generation and it is almost over. If we are going to do our job like the disciples of the first Church, we must do it NOW with so much urgency that we will get the grain gathered before it is too late!

Chapter 4

Unity—What Does It Mean?

In Ephesians 4:11 Jesus said, "*And He Himself gave some to be apostles, some prophets, some evangelists, and some pastors and teachers, for the equipping of the saints for the work of ministry, for the edifying of the body of Christ, till we all come to the unity of the faith and the knowledge of the Son of God, to a perfect man, to the measure of the stature of the fullness of Christ.*"

What have we been doing? God has appointed some to be apostles, teachers, pastors, prophets and evangelists but we are duplicating each other's efforts.

We are going into the same area with all of us doing our own little thing.

The apostle is doing his thing!
The teacher is doing his thing!
The evangelist is doing his thing!
The pastor is doing his thing!
The prophet is doing his thing!
We are all spending money!
We are all spinning our wheels not accomplish-

ing that which needs to be accomplished at all, but sometimes building little kingdoms of our own.

What is God saying to the body of Christ? Is there a possibility that we could come together in unity?

We don't believe there will ever be a time when the entire body of Christ will agree on denominational doctrine.

But is that important when compared to the value of souls?

We know what the Bible says about doctrine and that it is important, but are we so hung up on our doctrines and denominations today that we cannot lay down our differences to accomplish what Jesus told us to?

Is there any way that every ministry in the United States could join together and say, "I believe that I can lay down my doctrinal differences with you, my brother, to accomplish the one thing that Jesus said. Jesus came not to condemn the world, but *He came to seek and to save the lost.*"

Every program in every church should point to this one thing.

If it was worthwhile enough for God to send Jesus to the earth to do all the things He did, including dying, going into hell, and then being resurrected, then surely it is important enough to focus in like a laser beam on the same purpose for which He came; that purpose being to save the lost.

As a child, my brothers introduced me to a very exciting experiment. We broke the bottom off of a milk bottle so we would have a curved surface. By holding this glass in a certain position, sun rays would focus on a piece of paper with such a small condensed light spot that it would set the paper on fire.

That's what we want to see with the body of Christ. Have the purpose and direct light of God directed to such an exact spot that we will all be spiritually set on fire for the works of Jesus!

We may not be able to unify doctrine, but Jesus didn't say anything about that.

In fact He didn't come here to establish doctrines.

He simply preached the simplicity of the kingdom of God.

He came *to save the lost!*

But if we will all look above and beyond the doctrines, and that doesn't mean to drop all of our doctrines because they are all good in some ways and yet they're conflicting, but to drop them as far as the prime focal point of what Jesus is saying to do, then we can accomplish the preaching of the gospel to every creature on earth. Then we can make disciples of those people who are born again and send them forth for the same singleness of purpose — to save the lost!

So many times we have tried to consolidate two or more denominations hoping to bring a unity in that way.

That is not the way it will be obtained, because every denomination believes in their own doctrine. That's not wrong, but it's not the ultimate purpose of what Jesus said.

Actually if we will consolidate for a single purpose, not for a single doctrine, not for a single denomination, then we can obtain that single unity of *purpose.*

That single purpose is why Jesus came to earth.

That single purpose is how can we unite totally in one accord to do that one thing, preach the gospel to every creature on earth so that they can know Jesus.

John 12:46-48 says, *"I have come as a light into the world, that whoever believes in Me should not abide in darkness. And if anyone hears My words and does not believe, I do not judge him: for I did not come to judge the world but to save the world. He who rejects Me, and does not receive My words, has that which judges him — the word that I have spoken will judge him in the last day."*

Let us remind you again — Jesus did not come to hold campmeetings!

Jesus did not come to hold Harvest Celebrations!

Jesus did not come to hold praise and worship symposiums!

Jesus did not come to hold marriage seminars!

Jesus did not come to hold spiritual warfare conventions!

Jesus did not come to hold seminars or conferences!

All of these things are good, but they're not the central focus of what He said to do!

He came to seek and to save the lost, which should be the motive, the purpose and the main drive of every church, every evangelist and every Christian who is operating in the world today.

Remember we just said for a single purpose, not a single doctrine. If we would have all of these things that were just mentioned to you, that's wonderful, but each operation should ultimately come to that one purpose. . .witnessing and ministering to every person we can reach.

We are seeing a great unifying of the church on earth and we also believe God is starting to unify ministries as well.

This does not mean that ministries will merge their organizations, but rather they will unite for a single purpose.

There are many ministries with some of the facets of ministry utilized in Honduras for the great national evangelistic census which could have better been done if these ministries consolidated their people, training materials, finances, equipment, contacts, abilities, etc.

We see this unification of ministries becoming a merging for *purpose.*

Many international and national ministries cooperated with us, but not to the extent we see in the future.

We believe we will see many ministries coupling their "attack" on whole nations, consolidating their talents and purposes so nations can be covered with the gospel in a month or two of organization, preparation, and training, and then in two weeks these whole nations will hear the gospel.

This must be done in some methodical, systematic way so that we don't have gaps and miss people by the millions or even by the billions.

We must find the way that we can work as a team.

In the fourth chapter of Ephesians, God was speaking of one body, with all the parts necessary and all working in unity.

If you tried to put both feet forward at one

time, it would be an awkward way to walk.

That seems to be what the body of Christ is trying to do!

Each one going our own way, doing our own thing, in our own area and missing the in-between areas and missing the final purpose.

If we have a youth group, their purpose should be to save the lost and to make disciples of those.

If we have a senior citizens or a singles group or even a children's group or a married couples group, whatever groups that may meet together, they should go on with their Bible studies, their cell groups, their plans or programs but everything should focus and be directed to what Jesus is targeting for in this very decade.

John 14:10 says, "*Do you not believe that I am in the Father, and the Father in Me? The words that I speak to you I do not speak on My own authority; but the Father who dwells in Me does the works.*"

Jesus is saying that it is God who does the miracles through Him.

Jesus gave us that wonderful promise in John 14:12, "*Most assuredly, I say to you, he who believes in Me, the works that I do he will do also; and greater works that these he will do, because I go to My Father.*" Verse 13, "*And whatever you ask in My name, that I will do, that the Father may be glorified in the Son.*"

Jesus was saying that He would do whatever we ask Him, not so we could have a new Cadillac, not so we could have a new house, not so we could buy $10,000 dresses and suits that cost $2,000 for the husband, but for the one reason only, that the Father might be glorified in the Son.

At a recent meeting a girl said something very interesting and thought provoking. She said if you got up and announced to every person in your church that the Hunters were giving away a brand new Cadillac for $1.00, what would you do?

We all know the answer.

You would immediately run down to where the Hunters were giving a brand new Cadillac for $1.00.

You would also tell all your friends so they could take advantage of this great big deal that was going on.

Now stop and think, do we do the same thing for Jesus?

Do we do the same thing and go out and tell all of our friends, "You ought to come down to this meeting because they're going to teach you how to be a soul winner. They're going to teach you how to lead people to Jesus."

Or do we say, "Well, I don't think they would be interested in coming to something like that?"

Remember that $1.00 and the Cadillac analogy can be a tremendous tool to use to encourage people to do the things they ought to do so we can complete the task Jesus told us to do, which is to go out and to win the world for Jesus.

I often wonder if Jesus gave us a million dollars or bring it down to $10,000 or even bring it down to $1,000 for every soul we put into the kingdom of God, how many of us would work furiously to get the job done?

I have a feeling a lot of us would do a lot more than we are doing right now.

We have had a lot of wonderful teaching on prosperity.

I know that God wishes every Christian could be a millionaire and have all the things they ever desire, but unfortunately God can't trust most of mankind.

When He gives money, it's often used for the wrong purpose.

He blesses us financially so that His covenant may be established around the earth, and not so we will spend it on frivolous things.

How are we going to do all those things that Jesus set forth as a pattern?

How are we going to take the simplified part that we've given you in the paragraphs above and convert them to an actual operating method for this last decade to accomplish all that He said to do.

What did He say to do?

Preach the gospel to all five billion people on earth so that none, having the opportunity to hear the gospel, would perish!

He said it would be done by believers doing signs and wonders but He also said that every person would hear the gospel.

How are we going to determine that every person has heard the gospel?

Let us share a sample that God gave us to do in the nation of Honduras, in Central America.

Let us show you what can actually be accomplished by people who really get a vision.

Chapter 5

Honduras—A Nation Chosen By God!

A couple in Bradenton, Florida, Tom and Phyllis Reinecke, who operated a dry cleaning business (nothing especially spiritual about that), bought and watched our video tapes on How To Heal The Sick.

It totally and completely turned them on when they realized that the ordinary believer can lay hands upon the sick and see them recover!

It so stirred them, that they invited some of their neighbors to come the following week and watch the video tapes with them.

Their neighbors really got turned on and they immediately began laying hands on the sick. This encouraged this particular couple and they turned around and had another video healing school in their home.

This continued until they had held more than 26 schools. When they saw how people responded and got turned on, when they realized that Jesus meant it when He said, "*The works that I do will you do also and even greater works will you do because I go to be with my Father*" they decided to share it above and beyond where they were in their own little neighborhood.

Several years prior to that they had been to a church in Honduras, a very small, a very poor church, but a church that was enthusiastic about hearing the gospel.

They called our office to find out if we had the video tapes translated into the Spanish language, which we do, so they bought a set and called this pastor and asked him if he would like to have a video healing school in his church, after telling him all the exciting things that had happened in their lives as a result of 26 video healing schools.

They went to Honduras to hold the video healing school in *one* church.

The people got so excited about the fact that they could learn how to heal the sick even though they weren't educated, and they didn't know a lot about the Bible! They discovered that once they had the power of God they could lay hands upon the sick and see them recover.

Before this couple came back to the United States they had been to over 100 churches with this one little set of video healing tapes, teaching the people and letting them do the same thing as they were doing, which was laying hands on the sick and seeing them recover as a tool to get people to believe in Jesus and be saved.

One of the pastors said to him, "Do you think the Hunters would be interested in coming to Honduras?"

Tom said, "You have not because you ask not" and he added, "Let's call them."

They called us and God quickened our spirits and we said, "Yes, we would love to come to Honduras."

We immediately began sending video and audio tapes and thousands of books to Honduras to teach the people how to heal the sick, and a miracle started!

During the training schools, a student was given the opportunity to minister to a medical doctor who had been born with his feet turned under so he walked on his ankles, even as he practiced his medicine. All pain instantly left; and by the next morning his feet were perfectly normal for the first time in his life!

He is now not only practicing medicine, but is holding video healing schools, training believers how to do the same things Jesus did and that we would do.

We had never been to Honduras.

We're not famous and we don't have a television program.

Who knows who Charles and Frances Hunter are?

Nobody! Except those people who had watched us on the video tapes.

At first we were sort of "guess-timating" and I said, "I think we'll have 1,000."

Then we decided between the two of us that we might have 5,000. We thought, "Wow! That's really good!"

I said, "Oh, come on, let's just double it! Let's ask for a double portion. Let's believe God for

10,000 people for our first meeting in Honduras."

We excitedly left for Honduras to hold a Healing Explosion.

We were excited because of the tremendous hunger in the hearts of these people and because of the cooperation of the pastors there. There were over 6,000 people trained to be on the healing teams before we got to Honduras!

When we landed at San Pedro Sula we were met by two policemen. They were standing at the foot of the airplane steps and the afternoon sun was behind them. We could see that they were holding a picture in their hands.

It happened to be a picture of the two of us which had appeared on the front of a Charisma Magazine with our names underneath it.

They looked at the picture, they looked up at us.

They looked at the picture, they looked up at us.

They looked at the picture, they looked up at us.

When we reached the bottom step they said, "Are you Charles and Frances Hunter?"

The first thought that came to our minds because they had guns on their side, was, "What did we do wrong?" I think that same thought comes into the mind and into the heart of everyone of us, when we are in a situation like that, "What did I do wrong?"

It was very difficult not to admit who we were since they had our picture with our names underneath. So we said, "Yes, we're Charles and Frances Hunter." They said, "Follow us."

When a lady policeman and a man policeman have a gun, I guarantee you that you will follow them without asking questions! So we followed them.

When we got inside the airport, the policeman took Charles one way and the lady policeman took me another way.

Charles was taken out to the parking lot of the airport. When they got out there, the policeman led Charles to a station wagon where a man was lying down.

Our plane was two hours late. The temperature was probably 115 degrees in San Pedro Sula and this poor man had been laying out there for two hours. The stench was terrible — not only from the cancer, but from the heat! The policeman looked at Charles and said, "This man is dying of cancer — HEAL HIM!"

Charles did what Jesus said to do because we believe that, *"Those who believe shall lay hands on the sick and they shall recover."*

Charles cast out the spirit of cancer, commanded every cancer cell in that body to die in the name of Jesus.

After he had done that he spoke a new immune system into the man, commanded total healing, and left.

He saw no change whatsoever, but the Word of God says when we lay hands on the sick they shall recover.

The power of God was present to heal!

As he was going back into the inside of the airport, they put a blind woman in front of him and he laid hands on her. The first words she said were,

"You have white hair, you have white skin and you have the peace of Jesus on your face."

God had touched her eyes.

The power of God was present to heal!

Then they brought Charles to me. They had taken me into the Executive's Club where I thought they were going to give me a cold drink or something like that but I got the shock of my life to discover that the room was filled with sick people.

All kinds of sick bodies.

All kinds of diseases were present there.

They asked me to lay hands on them.

We began to lay hands on them and when we had finished with everyone they took us and put us back on a plane to go on to Tegucigalpa, the capitol of Honduras.

I thought, "Wow! What a way to enter a country!" Isn't that the way every Christian ought to enter a country? They ought to know you're coming with the power of God right in your hands! Hallelujah!

When we got off the plane in Tegucigalpa, the first thing they told us was the "good" news that the soccer team had come to town.

We had rented the soccer arena for Friday night. They said, "The soccer team is playing Friday night, so you'll have to have your meeting on Saturday night."

GRRRoss!

All of our advertising said Friday night!

Immediately our estimates of 10,000 went back down to the original 1,000. I'm not sure that either one of us thought there would be even a thousand people there.

Then we discovered they have lots of board meetings in Honduras. They said, "We have some meetings arranged this afternoon."

We said, "Fine."

They said, "We have some things we must discuss about the Healing Explosion."

They took us to the first board meeting and gave us a little kool-aid and some kind of little Honduran "goodies." Then I learned that there are some very famous words in the Honduran language. "By the way." I learned that "by the way" means "as you are going". . .by the way.

We didn't have any board meeting.

There was no discussion of the Healing Explosion whatsoever. We just had these little "goodies" and as soon as we were finished they said, *"By the way,* we have a woman who's dying of cancer, and a man who's also dying of cancer. Would you mind going in the bedroom and laying hands on them?"

Of course not.

We walked in there and laid hands on the woman.

She didn't look too bad.

We commanded the spirit of cancer to come out and spoke healing in Jesus' name.

Then we looked at the second bed.

We never saw anybody who looked more dead in our entire lives than that man did!

He was so shriveled up he didn't look like he weighed 60 pounds. He was nothing but skin and bones.

We charged over there because the Word of God says, *"Those who believe shall lay hands on the sick and they shall recover."*

We laid hands on him in the name of Jesus!

Sometimes faith may be small, but obedience is better than faith.

We laid hands on him like we had all the faith in the world.

I wasn't really sure I had faith at that particular moment, but I certainly had obedience!

When we got back in the living room, they brought in the whole back yard of people!

They had it loaded with sick people and one by one they strung them through the living room for us to lay hands on them.

The power of God was present to heal!

We finished that "board meeting."

We never did a bit of business except God's healing business.

Then they took us to the next meeting.

The first one happened to be in a middle class section.

The second "board meeting" was in one of the richest sections of town. And "by the way" meant exactly the same thing up on the mountain as it did down in the valley.

It meant, "We're loaded with sick people!"

This was a massive house!

They seemed to come out of the walls!

They came out of every room in the house.

Drug problems, alcoholic problems, back problems, head problems. . .you never saw so many problems in your entire life!

We just laid hands on them and the power of God was present to heal!

We saw incredible miracles.

A deaf mute girl about eight years old was

healed and as I had her repeat words after me, the people present laughed.

They said she had my accent which they thought was funny, but when you realize she had never heard anyone speak before she heard me, you can understand why she would pronounce words like I do.

We spoke at the Full Gospel Businessmen's Fellowship the next night and while we were there a telephone call came in and the caller said, "Tell Charles the man he laid hands on out in the car in San Pedro Sula was totally healed by the power of God and the doctor has released him and said he can go back to work on Monday!" Hallelujah!

The power of God was present to heal!

Then they said, "By the way, tell Frances that the little crippled boy she laid hands on in the airport who had never walked in his whole life is running and jumping! He's absolutely normal!"

That turned me on, too!

I thought, "One for Charles and one for me!"

Then came the night for the Healing Explosion.

We were positive we would have a small crowd but they have a communication system in Honduras that we don't have in America.

They don't have many telephones.

They don't have much television in their homes like we do so you can put an announcement on it. But they do have one of the greatest things in the world.

They have big mouths!

We got to the soccer field, anticipating 1,000 and got the shock of our lives!

There were somewhere betweeen 45,000 and

48,000 people there!

This is *after* the date was changed!

We had no opportunity to get out any publicity but word got around.

Why?

Because people talked!

That's the best advertising in the world.

More people in the United States should do more of it!

We estimated that more than 35,000 raised their hands to accept Jesus as their Savior and Lord and then more than 35,000 raised their hands to receive the baptism with the Holy Spirit.

As Charles ministered and they began to speak with other tongues all at one time, there was a sovereign move of the Spirit of the Living God like we never had seen in our lives.

When those people in Central America receive the baptism, they *know* it's the power of God.

We think, "Well, this could be the devil. My church says it's of the devil. My church says it's not for today. My church says that tongues passed away with the disciples." But praise the Lord, down there the people are so simple they will believe whatever you say from the Bible!

They don't pray quietly in tongues — they pray loudly in tongues!

We are not sure when we have ever felt more power in our lives then we felt as all of those people were praying in tongues.

They did not stop after fifteen or twenty minutes.

They just continued praying and praying and praying and praying.

As they continued praying, God did a sovereign work and people just got up out of wheelchairs, blind eyes were healed, people who were dying of cancer got up off of mats and began to run!

The meeting was covered by five radio stations, four secular and one Christian. They told us that on the secular stations the announcers wept all the way throughout the service.

The stations were on for five hours and they would say, "There's a man over there lying on a mat, he looks like he's dying."

Then there would be a pause and then they would say, "No, he's getting up and he's walking and he's running and he's leaping and he's praising God."

Apparently thousands were healed in this one meeting, with "*believers*" doing what Jesus instructed them to do.

These particular radio programs went all over Central America and the Caribbean.

Telephone calls were received for weeks afterwards from people saying that they had been healed just by listening to this service where the power of God was so strong.

Why?

Because the people were in one accord.

This was enough to make us super excited but that was not the thing that touched our hearts the most.

A meeting with 45,000 to 48,000 people is an incredible meeting.

When you see that many thousands of people get saved and get the baptism with the Holy Spirit that is another overwhelming thrill you just don't experience often in your lifetime.

But there was one thing that thrilled us more than that!

Many people can hear the Great Commission, many people can hear us speak on fulfilling the Great Commission, many people have heard thousands of evangelists and pastors speak on the Great Commission and they never get the vision of what Jesus told us to do.

But one pastor in Honduras really got the vision.

The motto of our ministry is, "If Charles and Frances can do it, you can do it, too."

This pastor began to think, "They said if they could do it, we could do it, too."

He decided he was going to try it.

The week following the Healing Explosion in Tegucigalpa, this pastor took 30 members of his church who had been through the video healing school and who had been a part of the Healing Explosion to a little town outside the capitol city. Tom Reinecke was the group leader. The village had approximately 400 people.

The pastor had said to them, "Let's look for a place in the town where we find the largest crowd."

The largest crowd they found was on the steps of the Catholic Church. There was a woman there teaching songs to little children.

They joined in and began to sing with them and when they stopped singing, one of the members very boldly said, "God sent us here to heal the sick. Is there anyone here who is sick?"

The teacher and three of the students were sick, so the team did what Jesus told us to do! They laid hands on the sick and they saw all four of them recover.

This brought quite a crowd of people and before the day was over they had a crowd of about 100 people! They preached the gospel to them and as we understand it, all of them accepted Jesus and many received the baptism with the Holy Spirit and many were healed.

At the very end of the day a little girl came to them and said, "My daddy is sick. He's dying of emphysema. Is there any way you could stay overnight and minister to him tomorrow because he's not here now but he will be here tomorrow."

The healing teams said, "Yes," and they stayed all night in the homes of some of the villagers there.

The next morning, bright and early, the family of this man who was dying from emphysema appeared at their door.

He could hardly walk two steps without gasping for breath because the emphysema was so serious!

The healing teams laid hands on him, commanded that foul spirit of emphysema to come out in the name of Jesus and the power of God went through this man from the top of his head to the tip of his toes.

He took a deep breath and screamed at the top of his lungs, "God healed me!"

He didn't stop!

He took off right then and there and ran up and down the streets (apparently the town is two blocks long). Here is a man dying of emphysema who has not been able to take two steps without gasping for breath, and suddenly he starts running down the street!

He ran two blocks down the street, circled the end of the village and ran back the other street screaming all the way, "God healed me, God healed me, God healed me!"

This had a tremendous impact upon the entire village because by the time he got back all 400 of the inhabitants of the village were there to see what had happened!

What an opportunity!

Remember that scripture said, "*Believe me because of the works you see me do.*"

The entire village came out and there was much joy in the city. The entire village was saved!

Acts 8:5-8, "*Then Philip went down to the city of Samaria and preached Christ to them. And the multitudes with one accord heeded the things spoken by Philip, hearing and seeing the miracles which he did. For unclean spirits, crying with a loud voice, came out of many who where possessed; and many who were paralyzed and lame were healed. And there was great joy in that city.*"

Talk about joy, there was great joy in that village because this man who was dying was healed! It was the miraculous which came into that little village that brought that whole town to salvation.

This pastor caught the vision of what we were doing and said, "If it works here in this one place, it will work other places."

This pastor caught the vision of what Jesus meant.

He had done what the Bible says for the five-fold ministry to do.

He had been through the video tapes and books

on How To Heal the Sick, he had trained his people how to lead people to Jesus, he had trained them how to minister the baptism, he had trained them how to cast out devils and heal the sick and handle the powers of the darkness. Then he did what Jesus told us to do, preach the gospel to everyone on earth.

He saw it.

He put it into effect.

He got a prototype of it.

It worked and it not only changed the lives of those people in that village, it changed the lives of the trained witness teams and it changed the life of his church!

That was a simplified model of the Great Commission and it worked just like Jesus planned.

This happened and was reported to us after we had come back to our home in Texas.

Shortly after that on March 31, 1990, we held a meeting in Austin, Texas sharing how to reach people for Jesus and how to train the believers what to do to become disciples of Jesus.

This little church was a year old and had about 150 members, about half of whom were children.

They trained their people with our video tapes and books and other training on how to lead people to Jesus and in two hours per Saturday for two weeks, they won 99 people to Jesus.

They actually won almost as many to Jesus as adults in their church!

They were excited when we came there because they knew our hearts and were excited about us sharing how to make disciples out of their people and all who came to the city-wide convention.

We were sharing this when God spoke something that we believe is the bomb that's going to explode and be a catalyst around the world!

God said, "Take a census of the world!"

We were talking recently on the subject of "How do you get faith without a doubt, then wish we wouldn't doubt that we had it!"

When God speaks to you and you know it's God, that's when you have faith without a doubt and can move mountains. (Matthew 21:21)

When God *says* something, you don't need any more faith!

You've heard Him, you know that you've heard Him, then all you need to do is run for it and obey!

That's what happened to us!

We heard God!

We knew it was God!

It was time for action — obedience!

Now — watch the action in Honduras!

In the United States we had just been going through our ten-year census.

We had been reading articles in the paper and hearing it on the radio and television and they were saying, "This must be the most accurate census ever taken in the nation."

They were saying, "Go under the bridges, go into empty buildings, but go find everyone who lives anyplace and register them as citizens or inhabitants of the United States."

This was very exciting!

We read an article in the largest newspaper in Houston. This article said that the government had hired 25,000 census takers, people of ordinary walks of life, paid them a typical clerical salary and trained them how to take a census. They showed them the census forms which were quite simple and how to fill them out and assigned each of these hired census takers a few houses.

Then they sent them forth to contact the people in those houses and to go back and back until they had finally registered everyone in each one in the homes assigned to them. This was probably about 25 to 35 homes because the average family has about three people in it in the United States. Twenty-five thousand were hired to reach approximately 2-1/2 million people in Houston.

With all this fresh in our minds we were saying, "Jesus is coming back. It won't be long!"

We all think it will be this decade!

Almost everybody on earth does.

The Spirit of God is speaking, is speaking, is speaking and we're hearing.

The body of Christ is beginning to hear what Jesus is saying.

They're beginning to believe what Jesus said will happen. Nineteen hundred and ninety years have gone by. Nineteen hundred and ninety years. Jesus said the gospel would be preached to all five billion people on earth.

In 1,990 years we're still going backwards. More people are being born physically than are being born-again and yet we get excited and say, "Jesus is going to be back this decade!"

His instructions to us, the believers, was that the gospel will be preached to every creature on earth, no exceptions, no missing ones. "I don't want anyone to perish," God said.

How can this happen? We said, "God, we know you are going to do something to change this whole pattern, this negative flow of ministry, of witnessing!"

What is going to happen?

We were at this little church when God spoke. It was toward the end of a morning service and I couldn't even tell Frances until the afternoon service because we were eating lunch with a group of people. But God said it as plainly as I have ever heard God speak.

He said, "Take a census of the world." He was speaking to the entire body of Christ. "Take a census of the world."

Jesus spoke it in slightly different words.

He could have said, "Take a census of the world," but instead He said, "Preach the gospel to every creature on earth" a direct parallel.

Jesus had put this in writing as His last words before He left this earth, as His last instructions to us to do the job that He had started!

This was a very simple model that would work whether we had a million people on earth or had five billion or more people on the earth.

When Jesus said, "The gospel will be preached to every creature on earth," those words cannot fail! Jesus spoke them into existence as much as God spoke the earth into existence!

These words echoed down through the centuries and have landed on earth for this very decade. We have been blessed. We have been chosen for such a time as this!

It must come about!

It cannot fail.

It *will* come about!

And we believe this is the decade in which it

will come about.

God was saying to us by using the word "census" that we were to reach every person on earth systematically, methodically so that we wouldn't overlap, we wouldn't omit anyone, we wouldn't duplicate.

We would go to them, but it wouldn't just be taking the names and information to register them as a registered resident of these houses, but God meant that we would go to every person on earth in our city, in our state, in our nation and in all the world and register everyone for the kingdom of God rather than as citizens of a nation!

Can this really happen today through us Christians of the twentieth century?

Why not?

God started census-taking and nations have copied His method to systematically count every person.

Jesus spoke this plan into existence in the Bible.

The Spirit of God has spoken the requirements into our minds and God, knowing we were aware of the way it was being done in America, simplified this whole plan by saying, "Take a census of the world!"

We must quit fantasizing and become realistic in accomplishing the fulfillment of the Great Commission within the next very few years. God could just wave His hand and accomplish this or He could send millions of angels, but God uses people to do the works of Jesus.

We can do it and because God and Jesus said it and planned it, it will be done!

God does not want a single person to perish, *"Behold, now is the accepted time; behold, now is the day of salvation"* (II Corinthians 6:2).

Do you realize He's saying now is the day of salvation through us to the world. I always thought, "That's the day of salvation for me." But He's looking out at the whole world and He's saying, "Today, this decade is the salvation date for the whole world."

Yes, we can do it if we'll go back to the way Jesus set up the prototype and follow His model!

The possibility is staggering; the potential is phenomenal.

The reality of this plan is within our reach this decade; the instructions of Jesus are plain.

Can every believer come into this Great Commission army under the combined leadership of all our ministries on earth today?

Can we call an emergency summit meeting of those who are already doing massive works of evangelization? Will you be willing to do this, just for Jesus?

This is not a ministry of Charles and Frances Hunter, or Billy Graham, or Campus Crusade for Christ, or the Southern Baptist Convention, or the Assemblies of God or other Pentecostal or non-Pentecostal denominations. It is a combined ministry of all believers working in unity under the plan God and Christ Jesus have written and now revealed to us for this last decade of harvest.

It is possible that the census ordered by Caesar Augustus was the first "*all the world*" census ever taken, ushering in the beginning of the New Testament when Jesus was born.

Is it possible that this "*census of the world*" is the way God wants to wrap up this era when Jesus will return to earth?

God has said to us, and probably to every leader in the world, "What you do, do quickly!"

Jesus said that to Judas in order to finalize the Old Testament and start the New Testament; now He is saying the same to us to finalize the works of the New Testament in preparation for *His arrival! Hallelujah!*

All of us must move rapidly into this final day of harvest and we solicit your call or letter to let us know your desires, vision, willingness to do this census-like world witness!

We need to know who God wants to use to organize this "preaching the gospel" to the five billion people on earth — this decade!

The body of Christ is scattered and shattered in multitudes of denominations. Now is the time to come together as a unified army — one single army to wrap up this age.

The whole world is being prepared by the Spirit of God for this great census-type evangelization.

We came back to our home in Houston and had stacks and stacks of work on our desks to do.

We had gone back to Honduras to the second largest city, San Pedro Sula and held the second Healing Explosion and the same thing happened there as in Tegucigalpa.

Probably 80% of the audience of some 25,000 to 30,000 were saved and received the baptism with the Holy Spirit and multitudes were healed through the hands of believers.

We simply walked around the inside of the stadium which was enclosed by a wire fence and we saw the hands reaching out as though reaching for Jesus.

Even as we touched them they were healed of blindness, paralysis, palsy and broken bodies!

Shortly after this trip to Honduras God spoke again.

This time to Frances.

Sitting at her desk on Tuesday, May 29th, 1990, God spoke and said, "Go back to Honduras on Thursday and set things in motion for the first census ever held in the world where a nation has the gospel preached to every creature in the country!"

Our desks were piled with work which needed to be done, but one thing we have discovered is that you never disobey God!

We called the airlines and were blessed with available tickets, got our clothes washed quickly from our last trip and by Thursday morning we were on our way!

The telephone lines buzzed between our office and Honduras on Wednesday, and the most exciting thing was that God had spoken in Honduras at the same time.

We asked our Honduras National Administrator, Luis Sorto, who is also our interpreter, to call a pastors' meeting on Saturday at 2 p.m.

God had already spoken to him and he had already called the meeting without any communication with us!

Our communication line was God!

On a three-day notice this was a miracle because most churches don't have telephones in Honduras.

It has to be by word-of-mouth that the news gets out.

They heard about this meeting and over 250 pastors came with great anticipation.

We told them that God had said Honduras would be the first nation in the entire world to have the gospel preached to every single, solitary creature!

Never in the history of the world since the New Testament Church has this been done before!

Never, never, never has this been done in modern times before, and God said, "I want you to train teams to knock on every single door in that nation.

"Every house in the valleys.

"Every house on the mountains.

"I want a trained believer to go knock on every door so that every person in Honduras will hear the gospel!"

I said to the pastors, "Do you know what this is going to require? This is going to require something that you have never done before."

To walk out into the unknown where the faith of mankind has never tread, your faith must go beyond your mind.

I said, "Are you willing to lay down your doctrinal differences? Are you willing to lay down these things that we all fight over because one doesn't believe in baptism by immersion and another does, one believes in this and another doesn't believe in that?"

I asked, "Can we lay down those denominational differences or doctrinal differences and believe that one soul is far more important than any or all doctrines or denominations?"

Jesus did not come to build a denomination.

Every denomination has been started out of strife. No wonder we have so much fighting among all of our denominations!

I was standing on the stage and said, "I want to show you what I mean. We've got to link arms with every other brother or sister in Christ, regardless of what their doctrine or their denomination is; we've got to lay that down."

I said, "Can you lay it down so we can link arms and accomplish what God wants to accomplish? Jesus only came for one purpose — to save the lost. Can we unite as one to accomplish His single purpose?"

I looked at the person next to me and asked, "What denomination are you?"

She said, "Catholic."

I asked, "Can a Catholic join arms with a Charismatic?" She was my interpreter.

She said, "Yes."

You don't know how the Protestants and Catholics fight in Latin America!

I looked over at the next man and asked, "What denomination are you?"

He answered, "Dutch Reformed."

I asked him, "Can a Charismatic join arms with a Catholic who will join arms with a Dutch Reformed?"

He said, "Yes!"

I asked the next pastor, "What church do you belong to?"

He said, "Nazarene."

I asked, "Can a Charismatic join arms with a Catholic, who will join arms with a Dutch Reformed, who will join arms with a Nazarene?"

"What church do you belong to?"

The next pastor said, "Assembly of God."

Now we had an Assembly of God standing next to a Nazarene standing next to a Dutch Reformed standing next to a Catholic standing next to a Charismatic. Can we link arms and forget our doctrinal differences so we can accomplish the Great Commission of the Bible?

Every pastor there, without exception, linked arms and said, "Yes, we can do it!"

That was the beginning of a united force in Honduras for a single purpose — not a single denomination or doctrine.

At the time of this writing about two months before the census begins, the best estimate is that 95% of all the pastors in the nation are united for this great move of God.

If Honduras, a model, prototype nation can do it, any city, state, or nation in the world can do it!

Chapter 6
Unity of Ministries

We began to have calls, letters and literature come to us because of the interest in the census-type evangelism as other organizations around the world observed that we are announcing what God is doing for Honduras.

This is the way we believe the Holy Spirit is working.

We discovered a tremendous move of God.

We have known about Campus Crusade all of our Christian life and have worked with them in many different ways.

Frances used the Four Spiritual Laws the first two or three years of her ministry to just simply lead people to Jesus.

It's a wonderful tool and can be used by anybody who would like to and it works!

We said, "God we need to get in touch with Bill Bright, the leader of this great organization and talk to him about it."

We said, "God will you cause him to remember who we are when we contact him and let him be receptive to this idea and coordinate it with his vast world-wide operation."

Would you believe that about a week later we were in Washington, D.C. on the opposite side of the nation from where he lives and half way across the nation from where we live.

We were in a van sitting directly in back of Bill Bright!

We only shared very briefly and said, "Bill, how would you like to see 25,000,000 witnessing Christians go out like a bunch of locusts across the United States and in two weeks time see millions accept Jesus until the gospel has been preached to the whole nation?"

The next morning we shared with him a little longer and shared this basic concept with him. Bill shared a plan for Campus Crusade For Christ. He said, "We're training 54,000 witness teams to saturate cities. By July of 1991 we plan to take major cities of the United States and go house by house sharing the gospel." Does this sound familiar with what God said, "Take a census of the world?"

It's being done by his organization at the same time other organizations are touching the same city.

We began to hear pastors say, "I'm going out house by house in my neighborhood." Or some of them have said, "I'm taking the city house by house."

Then we got literature and a cassette tape from Dick Eastman's organization called World Literature Crusade (Every Home for Christ). We were overwhelmed and amazed at how he has been doing this for decades.

We were astounded that he was doing a work

very similar to what God said to the church through us.

He has already got his plan organized.

He's setting it up for training of different churches to take this training with all of their people and move out into the neighborhood house by house, in effect doing a census of that neighborhood or that area of their city.

Why reinvent the wheel? Why not unify ministries?

We began to look at Ephesians 4:11 and saw something that God was showing us. I want to quote this scripture from the Every Day Bible. This is Ephesians 4:16: *"The whole body depends on Christ. And all the parts of the body are joined and held together. Each part of the body does its own work. And this makes the whole body grow and be strong with love."*

Did you notice how that's bringing the whole body together but it also implies that ministries will be joined together?

We see a unity coming in the purpose, not the denomination or organization, but the purpose of what we are to do.

That purpose again is focused on leading people to Jesus and making disciples out of them.

What about ministries?

We're going about doing our own thing and doing good jobs of it like Campus Crusade, like the 700 Club, like World Literature, like Billy Graham's organization and many, many others.

Each one of us doing a great work.

Some holding mass evangelism crusades.

Some setting up cell groups like Pastor Cho.

Many people all over the world are sending missionaries out to do work and we are all grappling for our own little part under each denominational leadership.

What would happen if we could find a unity of faith as it says in the 4th chapter of Ephesians and join the work of different ministries.

This would not change their organization nor would they lose their identity.

They would continue their work but instead of working separately they would join so that each one could become one part of the whole body until we could go take a nation with several of the ministries working together.

Would such a unity be possible the way the structure of the body of Christ is today?

We have recently heard that Pat Robertson through CBN (Christian Broadcasting Network) spent about 1.5 million dollars in Guatemala and El Salvador.

This was to make a television blitz over these two entire nations.

This was tremendous. It was an outstanding job and they estimate that probably 2,000,000 people accepted Jesus as their Savior and Lord!

But this still isn't doing all of what Jesus planned.

As great as this many souls were, what about the people who have no television sets?

What about the people who have no electricity?

What about the people who have no way of tuning in at that particular time?

Or failed to tune in.

Are they going to be left out and not included in

the gospel being preached to every creature, and what about follow-up?

We also understand at this time that Pat Robertson through Christian Broadcasting Network is doing a blitz in Argentina, spending approximately 1.3 million dollars.

Again, this is going to bring a tremendous harvest, but let us ask a question.

What would happen if all of us who are involved in ministry of this sort would join together and say, "This month is the month for Argentina."

We would pool our resources, materials and personnel, each of us putting in what we anticipated to spend in our crusade or effort in that nation.

What would happen if we all went together to accomplish one nation at one time instead of all of us "shotgunning" all over the world and duplicating the money spent over and over again and still never completing the job Jesus said was to be done?

It seems that in every piece of mail we receive, and we seem to be on everybody's mailing list in the United States, plus the many magazines we receive, the central theme and the central topic of every magazine today is winning souls to Jesus.

This has been called the decade of harvest.

This has been called the decade of destiny.

This has been called the decade of soul winning.

We have heard many, many things about the years between 1990 and the year 2000.

Most denominations have some sort of evangelistic plan of one kind or another to reach portions of the world through what they are doing. Yet, think of the magnitude of what could happen if we could somehow or another unite for the single purpose and say, "Let's get the job done."

It will never be done until we unite.

We do not believe under any circumstances that the gospel can be preached to every creature by one ministry, one national television, one television station, one denomination.

It's going to take a combination of all of us!

When we were in Honduras at the first pastors' meeting we asked a very simple question. "Which is more important, your doctrine or one soul? Can we lay down our denominational differences and stand together in unity of purpose, that purpose being to preach the gospel to every creature?"

This is the only doctrine that every denomination of the world will agree to and that is what Jesus said, "To preach the gospel to every creature in the entire world."

Every other doctrine ever created by man is separate and apart from this, but this one doctrine is something that all of us can agree on 100%.

Now are we big enough as individuals to lay down our denominational differences and join together?

Can the Assemblies of God lay down their denominational differences with the Catholics, can the Catholics lay down their denominational differences with the Pentecostals, can the Methodists lay down their denominational differences with the Nazarenes?

We're only mentioning a few of these churches because we want you to see how different all the denominations are.

Are we big enough, do we love God enough that

we are willing to lay down those differences to do what God wants us to do?

Is God big enough to soften our hearts so that all of us regardless of our denominational beliefs can join together to accomplish the great task for which Jesus came to this earth?

He did not come to set up denominations.

He did not come to set up doctrines, He came to bring people into the kingdom of God.

Can you imagine the ulcers Jesus would have if He had this much turmoil among the denominational differences within His own body?

Jesus is the head of this body and all members are members of the body and so we believe we can prevent Holy Ghost ulcers (there's no such thing, of course) by uniting.

We see ministries which do not even have to change their doctrine or their identity.

They can work together for a common cause and we believe God is ready to do that now by His Spirit.

We believe that God is putting this into the hearts of so many people and we believe this because we're seeing other ministries contact us and say, "Can't we work together? Can't we do this?"

We believe that God is going to bring together, perhaps even before you read this book, multitudes of ministries to a workshop discussion of what can we do to zero in, to focus in on exactly what Jesus wants to do among all of us as one unified body.

What an awesome thing it is, but didn't Jesus say it would happen before He returns?

It's happening today and we don't want to be left out of it, do you?

Now, look at how God brought unity to Honduras ministries.

One of the most important things each Christian must learn how to do is to lead someone to Jesus.

A meeting had been planned from July 4th to the 10th, 1990 to teach people how to be an effective witness through the Billy Graham organization.

At each of the Honduran churches where we spoke we asked them to attend this meeting.

As we mentioned, we had worked with Campus Crusade for Christ 25 years before when I (Frances) was first saved and they had a tremendous influence on my life.

They have a mighty outreach all over the world, and after nineteen years of not seeing Bill Bright, when we met him in Washington, D.C. at the National Day of Prayer and told him about the census God had told us to take, our spirits united. He was excited!

We contacted Campus Crusade for Christ National Director, Professor Luis Cubillo Mendoza, in Tegucigalpa and had a meeting with him on Sunday.

We purchased 10,000 Four Spiritual Law booklets in Spanish to give to pastors to teach their people how to win others to Jesus!

The Full Gospel Businessmen are assisting, and churches are laying down their denominational differences for the purpose of winning souls to Jesus.

There are about five million people in Honduras, and we believe as many as two million or more can be won to Jesus in this two week census, and a weekly Bible study made available to mature these new babies.

Our plane had stopped in San Pedro Sula on the way to Tegucigalpa, and our new-found good friends there said we ought to have a pastors' meeting there on Monday when we came back through.

In two days they contacted pastors and we had over 200 at our meeting on Monday morning between planes!

Their cooperation and excitement was incredible!

God had spoken, and we returned to Honduras, setting up all the details for a complete evangelization of the entire nation of Honduras, the first nation in the entire world to have had the gospel preached to everyone!

As we watched the progress of the preparation and systematic planning of this great census of the first nation on earth where the gospel will be preached to every creature, we began to see some principles God set forth in the Bible coming before our eyes in panorama as it was being performed in Honduras.

It was at this time that we began to see that the pastors could continue with their individuality, with their own doctrines, with their own denominations and not try to change all of these but rather to have a single purpose in mind, that of preaching the gospel to every creature on earth and then to make disciples out of these people to go on winning people to Jesus.

God had revealed unity in a new dimension and His people were ready and anxious to take Honduras for Jesus!

We said to each other, "But this wouldn't work

in the United States."

And then we said, "Why not?"

This began our thinking about what God could do if all the pastors and the five-fold ministries in the United States would lay down their doctrinal differences for one single purpose. . .to reach the people for Jesus.

Could they link arms for a single purpose without looking at their denominations and ministries?

When we began to see it was a unification of purpose rather than a unification of doctrines, denominations or programs, it began to make sense according to the Word of God.

Pastors were all in one accord, looking as one team at the purpose for which Jesus came to earth.

The lens of God's great seeing-eye cameras were being focused on the same picture God and Christ Jesus viewed from the beginning: this time had no beginning or ending, but it was broken into eras of time and purposes.

We are moving into an important era in preparation for the return of Jesus.

The great tribulation lies just ahead and we must prevent all who will from going through this horrible time described in the book of Revelation.

Let's take a few pages to explain the mechanical principles of how this is being done in Honduras as a prototype model which can be reproduced in any nation, any state, any city, any village or any area of your city around your church.

It will work if we will apply the method Jesus designed, established and put in writing for us 2,000 years ago.

Look at the chart which follows and see how

we set it up so it would start with a lead pastor and, with our help it was done with the local people.

It is being done under the leadership of pastors but applying principles that would cause it to work without being restricted and encumbered by denominations or ministries trying to build a church, denomination, or ministry.

If we build the kingdom of God, God will build our churches.

So this whole principle of what Jesus is saying is to build the kingdom of God without regard to denominations, without regard to doctrine, to do it unselfishly but for the purpose of doing what Jesus said!

If we have a selfish purpose in building our churches or building our denominations or building our kingdoms, it will not work!

None of our kingdoms will last: they will all fall eventually but the kingdom of God will stand forever and ever.

Pastors and leaders found that the denominations were not important at this point, yet they continued to exist as they had in the past and continued with their normal operations, but now moving into a new spiritual excitement and singleness of purpose!

They began to find a point of unity, a point of cooperation where it would not change their particular work or ministry.

We were not trying to get the Catholics into a Protestant denomination.

We were not trying to get the Methodists to join the Baptist church.

We were not trying to get the non-Pentecostals to become Pentecostals, although the last chapter of

Mark shows its importance.

We were not trying to mold them all into one congregation.

We were simply there to do what Jesus said, to build the kingdom of God!

Chapter 7

What About Follow-Up?

We were talking with a friend who is one of the great leaders in training people as witness teams all over the world.

He said, "If you have 100% success in this venture and don't do anything further than that, you will have wasted your whole time and you'll be the laughing stock of Honduras six months later."

Our initial thoughts were that all of these people would be invited back to their various churches and would receive their training under the pastor.

That is the way we feel it should ultimately be done because God has appointed the pastor with the assistance of the evangelists, teachers, prophets and apostles to train and equip the believers for the work of ministry.

When we began to consider this for Honduras, it began to take on another aspect.

Many of the pastors in Honduras have had no formal training as pastors.

They simply want to go out and bring people in

and teach them all they can by reading the Bible, if they have one.

We understand that possibly half the population do not read or write. However, we believe at least one person in each home can read so they can study their New Testament.

A major part of them, if they go to church at all, go to churches where they get inadequate teaching and maybe even wrong teaching.

A great deal of denominational teaching goes into their hearts.

We understand that from great crusades (mass evangelization) that only 0.05%, one half of one percent, of those who accept Jesus will become active in a church!

We must find a more successful follow-up for maturing these new babies in Jesus, and to equip and train them to be productive disciples.

Up until now, evangelists have held mammoth crusades where maybe hundreds of thousands, even millions have attended and multitudes have accepted Jesus, and then the next evangelist comes along and the same people come back to the meeting and "get saved again."

Then the next evangelist comes along and the same people "get saved again."

In the final analysis, numbers saved are not as important as those staying true to Jesus. The new converts must be nurtured, matured, and finally sent out as witnessing disciples.

Can you imagine the failure Peter, Paul, James, John and the other apostles and disciples would have encountered with no follow-up training?

When the same people go back to crusades

month in, month out, or year in and year out but nothing happens to them after that, they might as well have not bothered going in the first place because the question remains, "Did they really get saved?"

This is the same principle as if one million people in the United States had babies and then these new babies were thrown in a ditch, we didn't feed them, didn't nurture them, didn't take care of them, didn't protect them from the elements. What would happen?

All one million of them would be dead within a very short period of time.

Exactly the same thing happens with these babies who are "born into the kingdom of God" but who are not followed up!

They die spiritually and fall by the wayside before they have ever had a chance to grow or to mature at all!

What are we going to do for follow-up?

This friend of ours made a tremendous suggestion.

He said, "Why don't you plant 50,000 or more cell groups in Honduras all in the two weeks period when the teams are taking the evangelization census?"

Our spirits leaped within us as he said this but then suddenly we realized that many of these teams are not really qualified to lead a cell group.

The plan that we are putting into action is this:

The census takers will go out in teams of two.

Each team will visit approximately 35 houses in the area close to where they live.

After they have preached the gospel, they invite the people to a cell group meeting at their home or a designated location, on a certain date.

The census takers who have been trained in this area will then immediately become a cell group leader under the umbrella or protection of a church, if there is one available.

It was not until very recently that we connected "cell" of a Bible study group with the "cell" of science.

We have a book called THE CELL produced by Life Science Library, by John Pfeiffer and the editors of LIFE, Time Incorporated, Stonehenge Book.

When the thought occurred to me that there might be some descriptive common thread in the Home Cell Groups and the "cell" as science sees it, we looked at just a few thoughts in the book:

"It was three centuries ago that Robert Hooke of London, while observing slices of cork under his primitive microscope, saw that they were made up of a vesicular structure which reminded him of a honeycomb pattern. He called these wall cavities "cells."

"In the 150 years that followed Hooke's discovery, scientists came to regard cells simply as little boxes that contained the stuff of life. By contrast, it is realized today that even the most primitive cell is an immensely complex and highly integrated piece of biological machinery in which every part plays an indispensable role for the maintenance of life. The cell is, indeed, less the container than the very fabric of life.

"The reader will observe the machinery of the cell endlessly at work, generating energy and building new materials through processes of an incredible subtlety and efficiency which occur nowhere but in living organisms.

"There is no life without cells. And just as life itself is diverse, so are the forms and functions of the cells that constitute life. Some cells live alone, as free-moving, independent creatures, some belong to loosely organized communities which move from place to place and some spend their lifetime in fixed immobility as part of the tissue of a larger organism. Whatever its form, however it behaves, the cell is the basic unit of all living matter. In the cell, nature has enclosed in a microscopic package all the parts and processes necessary to the survival of life in an ever-changing world."

Maybe all of these descriptive phrases do not apply to what we today term "Cell Groups", but a lot of them do.

In the example of Pastor Cho's 50,000 home cell groups, we understand that he operates them under the umbrella of his church, and that has been phenomenally successful in maturing believers.

As we began to think about Honduras, the prototype or model cell group plan appeared as the ideal plan to follow-up on the newly converted Christians, as well as further maturing others who had been born again before the census-evangelism to be held in January, 1991.

At first we thought about having the cell groups formed under the leadership and direction of the various churches of the many denominations in Honduras.

Questions began to arise as to how this could work properly when doctrines were involved which differed in every denomination, Protestants and Catholics, Pentecostals and non-Pentecostals.

Then we realized that many of the pastors in Honduras, as it is in other third world nations, have no formal training to be pastors.

The plan loomed before us that all of this could be settled by providing every cell group and every church with the same training tools in the form of audio or video tapes.

If half the population, as we were told, cannot read or write, they can listen to AM or shortwave radio all over the nation; most have an audio cassette player, and in some few cases can watch video.

We carefully studied what we had available in Spanish or could make available in the short starting time we had, the teaching must contain no denominational doctrinal views!

It must be very simple, everyday living, scripturally correct training suitable for all denominations.

We believe that as time goes on and other nations conduct a national census, and even future training in Honduras, other ministries will provide training they have developed which also can be used interdenominationally, but highly suitable for maturing the saints for the work of ministry.

By training with the same materials in every cell group and also in every church which will participate, the spiritual water level will be raised for the entire nation.

As these newly born-again believers, along with the more mature ones, gain knowledge of the word of God and the simplicity of how to live for Jesus, they will be invited to become members of various churches and denominations, all of which have had the same training.

We believe the Holy Spirit will then further their training in the churches under the leadership of pastors without our continued leadership.

The cell groups will not start under the leadership and umbrella of the pastors and individual churches, but every church and denomination will greatly benefit from receiving the new Christians as the Holy Spirit leads them to the various churches.

We initially felt that each of the 50,000 or more cell group Bible studies would need an audio tape each week for about thirty-six weeks.

When we began to make plans for reproducing this volume of audio tapes and video tapes to cover the entire nation, and then realized the vastness of distribution through the same chain of census teams, we saw the magnitude of this work and the tremendous cost involved.

It was overwhelming us and we were saying, "God, show us an answer to this" when we got a call from Ralph Turner, our representative from our office in Honduras who is supervising this entire operation.

Ralph said the Christian radio station there is astounding us with their willingness to say, "Use this station any way you desire."

They are providing us with programs any time we want them!

They are providing talk shows, unlimited radio spots, and even basically unlimited time on the radio station!

It was as if God made a complete radio station available just for this census evangelization of a whole nation.

He has so spoken to the hearts of the owners of the station that they're putting their whole effort into this venture. Suddenly it dawned on us, "Why couldn't we hold nation-wide cell groups by radio?"

What a powerful revelation began to appear before our very eyes and thoughts.

What if we had only one audio tape made of the teaching and played it on maybe two different nights of the week and have radio home cell groups where they would meet in homes or in a public place on that same night, listen to the radio teaching from our cassette tapes and then have a second hour where they discuss the program and carry it on as a normal cell group discussion and training.

This would give them all a chance to participate but they would be in a group instead of trying to listen to a radio at home.

We know if you have a systematic plan, people will attend.

It will be the job of the census taker teams to sell them on the idea of coming to these weekly meetings, and every future week to follow-up.

They should come to the first one thirty minutes early and discuss some of the things which will happen.

Have the radio ready to turn on and have their one hour cell group radio training.

We were amazed at the simplicity and economy of a national weekly radio cell group Bible study.

The audio tapes now will only cost about $2.00 weekly instead of hundreds of dollars. Hallelujah!

Isn't this an overwhelming concept for Honduras? Virtually everybody, even in little huts, even in the back woods, have a battery operated radio!

This is their basic means of hearing people.

Many of the houses have no electricity or running water.

When darkness comes they have nothing to do except listen to the radio or they can make an audio cassette copy of the radio Bible studies and listen to them at home over and over.

They actually have a golden opportunity to be able to listen to these Bible studies.

With the availability of radios within the nation, and multitudes of the people already listening, and then frequent announcements for the Bible studies, we can see well-attended cell group meetings.

This is going to, of course, increase the listening audience of this particular radio station and perhaps even other Christian radio stations in the nation, which we understand want to network the Bible studies.

What an overwhelming opportunity for radio stations to preach the gospel!

This teaching must be very, very simple.

We are careful to select teachings that are interdenominational, that are simply building and maturing the Christians from babyhood on up to miracle-working disciples.

It is an advantage to have a two-way communication, so they can phone into the radio station and ask questions.

The radio station will continue a second hour so they can have a central location for all the cell groups to attend.

Many of them don't have telephones!

Many have no money to make phone calls.

That's also a lot of people to be calling in one night.

But God did another miracle.

For political reasons, the government of Honduras made a telegraph machine available to even little villages of 20 or more people.

They have telegraph operators in all these little villages and cities.

When the government was having an election they could telegraph the results of the count of the election by Morse code and they could accumulate the count very quickly for the whole nation.

What an opportunity for God!

All of these cell groups will have access to a telegraph where they can send questions or comments by Morse code.

If they can't get their message in during the hour program, then it will be taken up the next week either during the week or at the next cell group night.

They can actually plan and work from a central headquarters where pastors and leaders can be a panel for discussions.

Testimonies can flood in and be shared either live from the Tegucigalpa headquarters or from some other radio station.

In all cases it will be made available to these home cell groups and all who desire in the whole nation can take advantage of this national cell group Bible study.

God has made this wonderful plan available to all of Honduras! Hallelujah!

Ralph and Joan came back to our Texas headquarters for a few days, and God opened our eyes to another phenomenal tool.

He told us there existed something he called a "black box." We purchased a pair of these "black boxes" for about $2,600.00.

What do these "black boxes" have to do with the Honduras national Bible study?

One will be in the central radio station; the other can be used anywhere in the nation where a telephone exists.

They simply plug this into the telephone mouthpiece and they can broadcast live from any city, town, village, or cell group meeting in the nation.

With this great little tool, each week different pastors and leaders will be enabled to participate live in the Bible studies, and allow those attending to ask questions and make comments!

Isn't God good?

We understand that the broadcast power for this station will be increased January, 1991, so the signal will reach *all of Central America* and a lot of the Caribbean islands and part of Mexico!!

At the time of this writing, we see action being taken for every Central American nation to take an evangelistic census during 1991.

God's uniqueness will enable all of Central America to conduct a weekly cell group Bible study attended by multimillions of believers — all for about $2.00 per week!!!

Thank you, Radio Station HRVC and other participating stations.

We want this training to be available to whole churches so that at the same time cell groups are meeting, every pastor can have a meeting on the same night in his church.

All the people in the nation can have church meetings along with the cell groups.

They will all be trained in a similar way and like filling a bathtub with water, the spiritual water level of the nation can be raised all at one time.

We believe that many, many ministries have Spanish materials which can be used.

We must carefully select the teaching to teach basic, nondenominational, scripturally accurate materials, teachings that will mature the believers, whether they are new converts or mature Christians.

We believe God will lead us to the proper teachers and materials.

These same people will then be going back to local churches.

At each cell group they should announce which churches are in the area.

Many thousands of villages have no church.

Pastors are already planning to establish churches in villages where there are none, arising out of the cell groups.

We are trying to stay away from every denominational aspect possible, but we believe the Holy Spirit will lead them into the churches where they can find further, healthy food.

If they go to a church which does not provide maturing scriptural messages for them, then they will simply be drawn by the Spirit of God to where they can hear the right teaching.

God has put a hunger in the hearts of these people until they want more and more of Jesus.

We believe these cell group Bible studies, new churches, existing churches growing spiritually and numerically will bring life to the nation until the whole nation will have the spiritual level brought up almost simultaneously.

We looked over the material we have in English and made a decision to put in Spanish a certain number of the hours, but with very, very simplified teaching such as How to Read the Bible, What is God's Part/Our Part; How to Hear God; Holy Living; How to Lead People to Jesus, and many others.

Recently Frances made a talk on the heartbeat of God. When we listened back to what she had said, it was overwhelming the amount of basic teaching that was given in that one lesson.

It draws people to the personal acquaintance with the Lord Jesus Christ until they can really know that it's not "I who live but Christ who lives in me."

That is the first chapter of this book, but will be on a Spanish audio tape for the cell group Bible studies by national radio.

This model in Honduras can be duplicated in all the Spanish world with the same tapes and tools. Church growth will be phenomenal!

Chapter 8

How To Mobilize And Evangelize A Nation

Pastors and a growing number of Christians are like seeds looking for fertile ground.

God has prepared the hearts of people all over the world, both sinners and Christians, for this great end-time revival where hundreds of millions, if not billions, will be saved.

Jesus lives in the very heart of every sincere Christian. He wants *souls* to present to His Father!

Think of the excitement in heaven as multiplied millions times millions are being saved!

When all the angels rejoice at the salvation of one soul, think of the rejoicing of angels when these mass multitudes are joining God's royal family!!!

Finally in these last days, God has revealed *His simple workable plan to reach these masses!*

We, the Christians of today, are blessed to be the ones chosen for this hour to make God and Christ Jesus rejoice with the riches of heaven — *souls brought into the family of God!*

When God spoke to us and said that Honduras would be the first nation to have every person evangelized, God had already provided the "man" for the job.

Ralph Turner watched our video tapes prior to the San Antonio, Texas, Healing Explosion and instantly caught the vision of what Jesus is saying to the body of Christ today and heard the call of God to join with us in this vision!

Ralph had received years of training in the Southern Baptist denomination and later in Charismatic churches, has held multitudes of positions, but all were preparing him for this great census-type evangelization of nations.

He and his wife Joan joined our ministry, moved to Houston, and then went to Honduras to remain there until the census is completed.

God has mightily and consistently given them favor with the leaders and people of Honduras, and he has established a rapport with pastors of virtually every denomination.

God has given him great wisdom as an ambassador for the kingdom of God.

Perfectly qualified leaders have poured into his assignment until it seems that at every turn of events, every challenge, every day God is performing miracle after miracle to accomplish His purposes in His perfect timing — all to culminate with the great census from January 5-19, 1991, and the Harvest Celebration on January 19, 1991.

God has a *plan* and a *man!*

Following is "The Plan" which worked in Honduras, and which will work in any city, state or nation in the world!

"The Plan"

by Ralph Turner

Even when God decides to move, it must involve a plan.

There must be people to operate that plan.

It was that way in Honduras.

When Charles first received the mandate to "Take a Census of the World", there was no plan.

Only a command.

However, as people began getting involved, the plan began to emerge.

This was a learning experience like never before.

How do you reach a nation in just two weeks?

It has been tried by many!

Denominations, independent groups, individuals with huge dreams, all have had the vision.

They have had the desire.

But there must be a plan.

There must be a plan that will include enough people to cause it to flow. . .and result in the desired conclusion.

The need for faith ceases when God speaks, and then all that's needed is obedience and action!

We instantly obeyed God when He said Honduras would be the first nation where the gospel will be preached to every creature.

Action was started immediately.

Following is how the Holy Spirit led us to operate the plan to evangelize the nation of Honduras.

CENSUS ORGANIZATION SCHEDULE

Stage "A"
(Figure No. 1a)

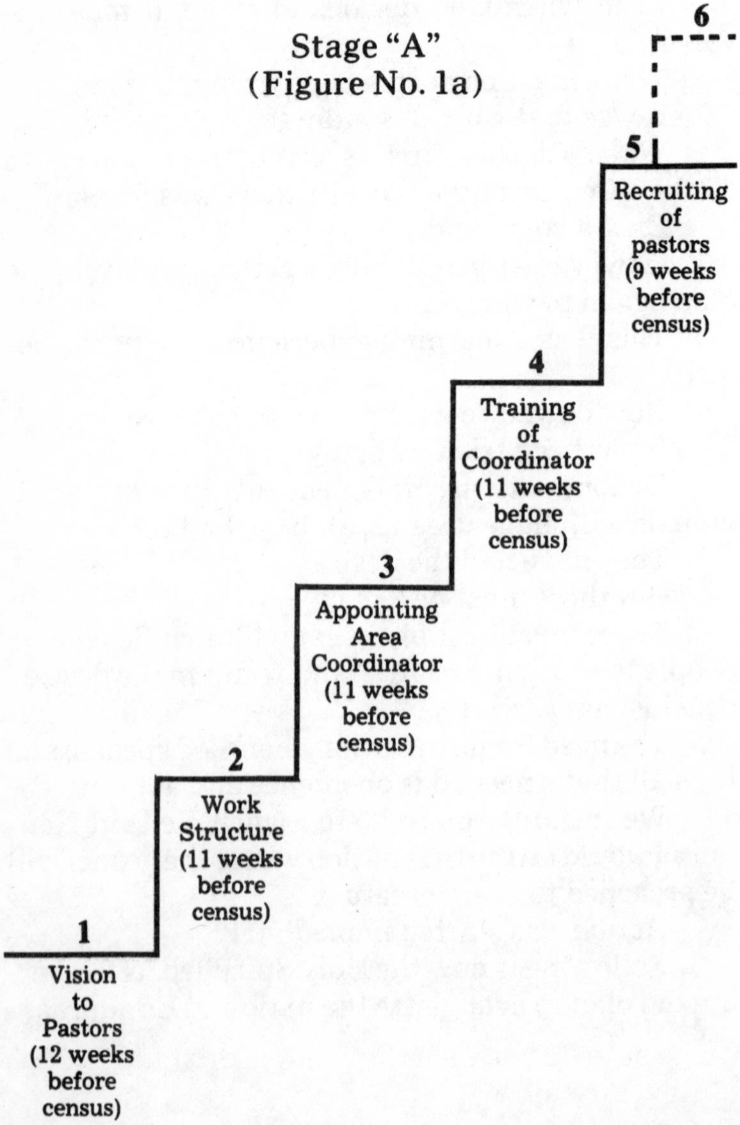

Stage "A"
(Figure No. 1b)

1. Pastors must catch the vision. Meeting should:
   a. Share the vision of census-evangelism.
   b. Encourage them to lay down differences.
   c. Work together to train their people to reach every home in their area.
   d. Watch the one hour video or listen to the one hour audio HOW TO REACH EVERY PERSON IN THE WORLD FOR JESUS
2. Work Structure:
   1. Pastor who is spiritual leader of census operation.
   2. National Coordinator to supervise phases.
   3. Assistant National Coordinator to make sure all usual work is being done.
3. Each area (in Honduras - departmento or state) must have one person to contact pastors, help him prepare for census, set up training in his church.
4. Each area coordinator must be trained in: how to relay the vision to others, how to help the pastor implement all the training into his congregation, how to distribute the materials, how to compile all results and return to central office.
5. Recruiting of area pastors is very important. Every part of the target area must be covered. Each pastor must accept responsibility for a certain part of the target area. The coordinator must be sure he has the vision and is commited to follow through.

The first objective must be to gain the support of as many pastors as possible. (See Figure No. 1a and 1b.)

This is paramount to the success of the mission.

The pastors over an area, be it a city, state, nation or the world can either open the door to the work of the Holy Spirit, or close it tight.

If there is to be a significant move of God at your location, then there must be a move of the Holy Spirit on the hearts of the local pastors for it to happen!

We first made contact with the head of each denomination which operated in Honduras.

We also communicated with the leader of every independent group that we could locate.

We needed to get them all together in one location.

Perhaps together they could really accept the challenge.

We invited them to all gather in the capitol city of Tegucigalpa.

We even offered to pay their transportation to the capitol and cover all expenses during their stay.

Most of those invited accepted.

There were some 25 different groups represented.

When we first began to consider our work in Honduras, we had become associated with a nationally known and respected pastor, Roberto Ventura.

He became our Honduran pastoral representative.

He opened the meeting.

This gave the meeting, and indeed the entire plan, a "local" flavor.

It was not an American ministry coming into a foreign land to do great things for the poor local population. When working in another country this can be very important!

Pastor Ventura welcomed the national pastors to the meeting. Then he introduced a well-known business man, Emanuel Rodriquez who is the vice-president of the Full Gospel Businessmen's Fellowship in Honduras.

God allowed him to catch the vision of the evangelistic census.

He shared the concept with the pastors.

They listened.

They began to see the possibilities.

Then Luis Sorto, a young Honduran who began as our interpreter and was later appointed as the National Evangelistic Census Coordinator, explained to them as much as we knew at that time about how this event would be implemented.

At the end of the meeting, each pastor pledged the support of his group.

Each one then supplied us with a list of pastors from various locations within the country.

Pastors who they felt would be excited about the plan.

The next step in the plan was the formation of an "Organization".

ORGANIZATIONAL CHART (HONDURAS)
(Figure No. 2a)

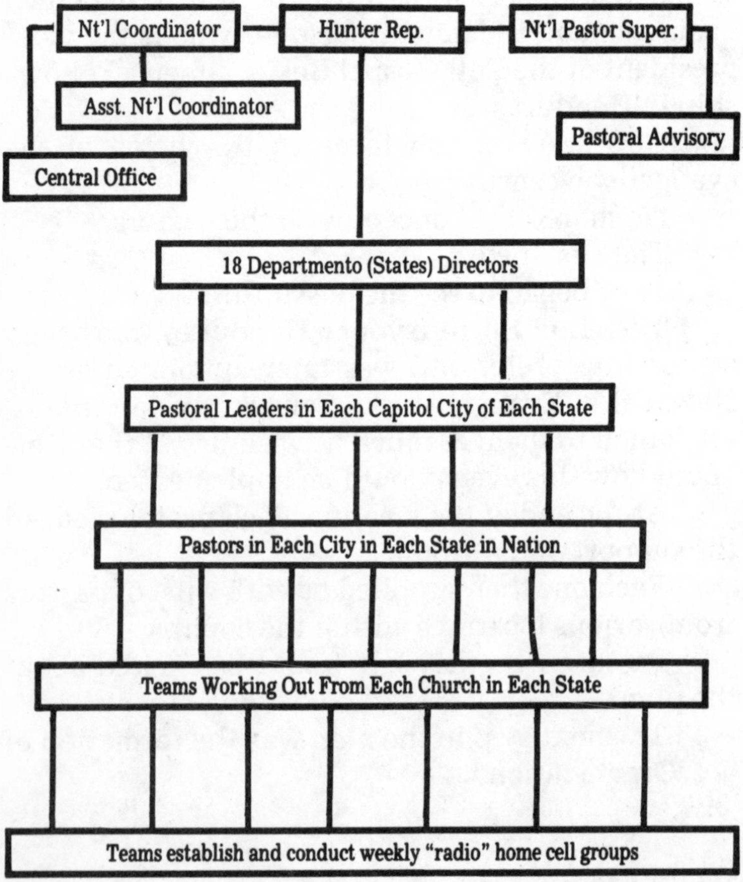

ORGANIZATIONAL CHART
(Figure No. 2b)

1. Executive Staff:
   a. Hunter Representative: Relays the vision given to Charles and Frances Hunter to those working with him. Handles the supervised budget and general activities. Serves in an advisory capacity.
   b. National Pastoral Supervisor: Serves as spiritual advisor to operation. Works with pastoral advisory board to relay suggestions to Hunter Representative and Director. Works with both to put into operation the various phases of the census.
   c. National Coordinator: Directs the implementing of all activities. Supervises the state Directors. Deals with advertisers. Sets up and coordinates national and local meetings.
2. Pastoral Advisory Board: A group of pastoral leaders who join together to offer advice on certain matters when requested. They have no decision-making power. The Executive Staff takes into consideration all advice given. But is not under obligation to put into practice those things suggested by this committee.
3. Central Office: Consists of secretary with volunteers as needs arise. Here all the results will be tabulated. Also is the point of contact for all those who work with the leadership.

4. State Directors: These are ministers directed by God for this work. Their job is to:
   a. Work with pastors in understanding the vision.
   b. Constantly recruit new pastors.
   c. Make sure all pastors have plenty of materials.
   d. Make regular reports to Executive Staff.
   e. Return all reports to the Central Office.
   f. Help tabulate all results.
5. Each state, as in Honduras, or each area as in a city must have its pastoral leader. Those who lead the way in the census. They will recruit other pastors and keep them encouraged. Generally they will not need to be appointed — they will just come to the forefront.
6. Each pastor who becomes involved is a very important part of the census. He will assume responsibility for a certain part of his town. He will train all possible in his congregation to take a part in the census.
7. Teams: Each team consists of two or three people. Each team member is trained on winning people to Jesus and making use of all the material provided. The team has the responsibility to make contact with every person living in his assigned area.

To begin this we needed an *Executive Staff.*

These consist of the ones who will direct all the activities from a central office in the capitol.

They must be people who are respected by the nation, have abilities that are needed to make the plan flow, and are able to spend a good deal of time involved in the workings of the census.

The staff consisted of Pastor Roberto Ventura as the Pastoral Advisor, Luis Sorto as the National Administrative Coordinator, Oscar Vasquaz working with the communication of the concept throughout the nation, Emanuel Rodriquez providing both business and legal advice; and Ralph Turner from the U.S.A., the representative for Charles and Frances Hunter who directs all activities of the Evangelistic Census, Harvest Celebration, and cell group Bible studies.

The nation of Honduras is divided into 18 states, or "departmentos" as they are called there.

We further divided the nation into three "districts", each containing 6 states. The northern district with its main large city of San Pedro Sula. The western district directed from the city of Santa Rosa. The southern district that would be watched over from the national capitol of Tegucigalpa.

There was no eastern district as that part of Honduras is very sparsely populated.

The next phase in the formation of our organization was to place within each district a director who was capable of guiding the activities in each state.

We would then need a person in each state who could serve as a *departmento director.*

His main function would be to do the "leg

work" in that state.

He must personally make contact with every pastor in his state and involve him in the census.

Following is how we located, and "set in", these vital persons.

There were three young men who had been very active in our Honduras Healing Explosions up to that time.

They had shown a lot of interest in becoming even more involved.

We assigned each of them to one of the three districts.

They were to go to the capitol city of each state in their assigned district and do three things.

1. Contact every pastor in that city.

2. Share the evangelistic census plan with them.

3. Announce to the pastors a motivational meeting to be held by one of three evangelistic census team leaders in the near future.

He was to:

(a.) Ask for one of the pastors to volunteer his church as the location for the meeting.

(b.) Tell the pastors of our need for someone to serve as the state director from that time until the actual taking of the census.

He was to interview all those who expressed interest in this job, and, following a list of requirements we had given him concerning the type person we wanted, invite any such person to a training session at our office in Tegucigalpa.

And so. . .on Monday morning they arrived.

They were to undergo eight days of intensive training! At first they were taught some very vital things about God's plan of salvation.

We talked with them about rebirth.

Then about how to lead a person to accept Jesus as their Savior.

Then they experienced the fourteen hours of video training on "How To Heal The Sick".

They were required to spend their evenings reading the textbook by the same name.

The last two days of classroom time were spent with such subjects as how to dress when calling on pastors, and how to talk to them.

They were given some valuable information on the proper use of an expense account.

Then they were shown exactly how to guide a pastor in getting his church ready for the Evangelistic Census.

On Saturday we assembled about 300 people in a church downtown.

We had advertised on the radio, inviting all who would like to be the first trained in "How To Be A Census-Taker" to be at the church that morning.

The newly trained Departmento Directors helped in that training by passing out the literature to be used and being available to give individual help to anyone who needed it.

Then we took all who would go to a small community just outside of town. (I say all who would go because during the class it began to rain. By the time we were ready to go to the community to take the "sample census", it was really pouring. However, about 65 people still went, anxious to be the first to test the "technique" we felt God had given us).

We arrived at the small village about 1:00 p.m.

It was still raining.

All the streets were dirt (mud now) and all the houses were situated on the side of a steep mountain.

It was really slippery.

The directors had been stationed at various places in the village.

Team members had been assigned to each one and they soon worked their way to where their "director" was waiting.

They then were sent to certain areas of houses, and very soon the "census" was under way.

It continued for about two hours.

Most of the witnessing took place inside the small houses and huts. The rain did have that benefit at least.

The people would not allow the census takers to stand outside in the rain and talk to them.

They would quickly invite them inside.

In the two hours we worked, everyone got soaked to the skin!

But. . .some 323 people were presented with the gospel of salvation. Two hundred and seventy-one (84%) invited Jesus Christ to come in and take over their lives.

The census-takers were supposed to meet back with their assigned director and turn in the census forms they had filled out on each person.

Many got turned in, but because of the rain, some of the witnesses went on back to their own homes without turning in the forms. The above results are based on those forms that did make it back to our office.

From the results, we felt that the Holy Spirit was giving us not only His approval of what we were doing, but just a hint of what was going to happen during the National Evangelistic Census!

The next phase of the plan was the sending out of these departmento directors to their assigned states. (See Stage A, Figures 1a and 1b)

They left the next day after the practice census.

They were to telephone at least every other day to give a report to the office on the progress being made in their areas.

Within a very few days each city was ready for the motivational meetings.

In several of the cities it was reported that every pastor in the city had pledged to come not only to the meeting, but to be involved in the census.

It was with a lot of excitement and expectation that the three teams left for the meetings.

One team was headed by Dale Proctor, an American missionary to Honduras who had begun to work with us to make this project a success.

Another was guided by Tom Reinecke, a retired businessman from Florida and the one God had used to introduce Charles and Frances to Honduras.

The third was headed by Ralph Turner, Charles' and Frances' International Ministries Director.

For nine days the three teams traveled.

Each night a meeting was planned in another state.

They would hold a meeting one night, then leave early the next morning to drive to the next state for the meeting that night.

All the meetings were successful.

The team would share the vision and how the pastors there could be involved so as to change their town and their nation.

Then the challenge would be issued and the team spokesman would ask the pastors to make a commitment to the Lord and to each other to work for the success of the census.

In every meeting *most* of the pastors in the town attended.

In several meetings *every* pastor in the town came.

In *every case* the excitement was high.

With these meetings, stage "A" was completed.

God's Holy Spirit was activating miracles unheard of on earth in modern times.

So far we had:

- Alerted the spiritual leaders of the nation as to what God was about to do in Honduras.
- Secured the support of most of the pastors in Honduras.
- Formed a very effective executive staff.
- Trained and sent out a director for each of the 18 states.
- Conducted an informational and motivational meeting in the capitol city of each of these states.

The Evangelistic Census of Honduras was off to a very successful start!

Jesus said, "*Go therefore and make disciples of all the nations,* | **HONDURAS Jan. 5-19, 1991**

baptizing them in the name of the Father and of the Son and of the Holy Spirit, | **Jan. 20, 1991**

teaching them to observe all things that I have commanded you; | **Starting Jan. 21, 1991**

and lo, I am with you always, even to the end of the age" (Matthew 28:19,20).

TRAINING

Stage "B"
(Figure 3a)

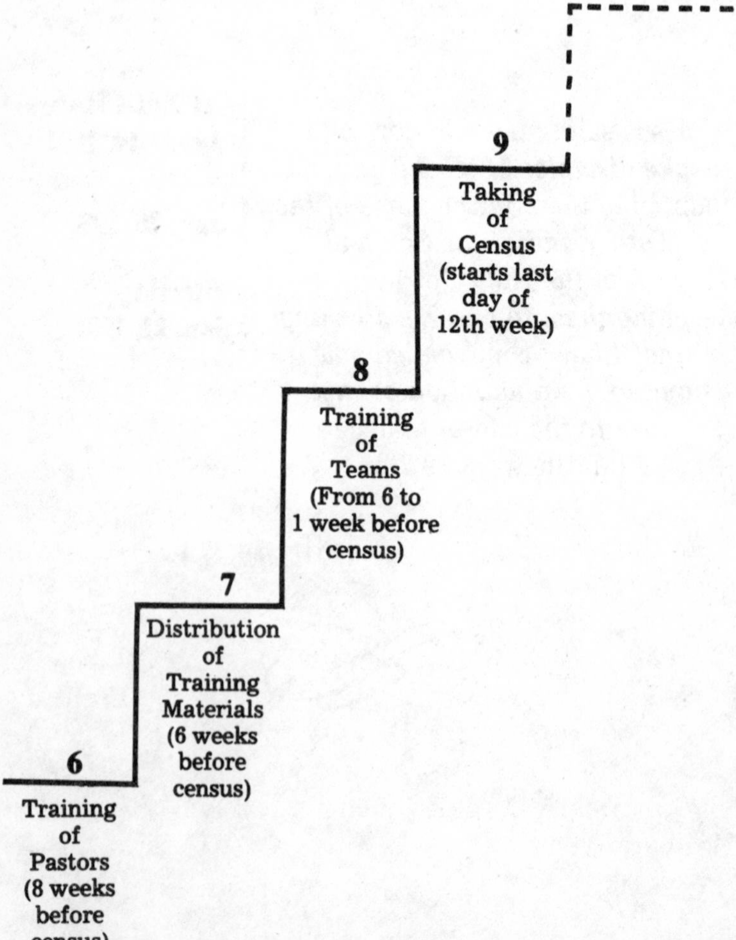

Stage "B"
(Figure No. 3b)

6. An audio tape is the tool that really prepares the pastor to get his church ready for the census. On it the vision (in Honduras) was shared by a national leader. Then the national director gave details on using the materials, training his teams, assigning areas, and doing his part of the census.

7. Here all tracts, Bibles, instruction cards, and all other training and census materials are placed into the pastors' hands. The pastor starts at once to have training sessions with his teams.

8. Each team member is taught how to lead a person to Jesus and how to fill out all the forms. They are assigned partners and the area of town for which they are to take responsibility.

9. Everything has been leading up to this point. Each team goes to their assigned area and begins to knock on doors presenting Jesus. Whenever they fail to get an answer, they make a note of it on the form and plan to return until they contact every person in their area during the two weeks. They make a report each day of results and turn in the census forms. All forms are returned weekly to their supervisors, and in turn go up the organization chain until they reach the central headquarters.

Entry into Stage "B" (see Stage "B" Figure 1a and 1b) started with the production of a "training tape". This 60 minute audio tape was designed to answer every question a pastor might have about just how he could get his church people ready to take part in the census.

It began with a recording of Charles announcing to the crowd at the San Pedro Sula, Honduras Healing Explosion that *God said, "Take a census of the world."*

Then Luis Sorto welcomes the listening pastors to the *Evangelistic Census* team.

Following that, one of the leading pastors in our work in the census, Pastor Alex Lanza, talks to the pastors heart to heart.

He shares what the census means to him, how it has put a new measure of excitement in his life, and what it means to the nation of Honduras.

He later volunteered four days a week to the census. He has a desire to help in all Central American nations to conduct evangelistic censuses.

Then Luis shares the "mechanics" of just how the census will be accomplished.

After this session, every pastor should be able to see just how he can mobilize his church to take part.

Finally, Frances shares one of the most dynamic and moving charges ever recorded.

She talks to the pastors just like Jesus might talk to them if they had been with Him just before His ascension back into heaven.

No pastor could hear this without being motivated to make a recommitment of his entire life and ministry.

A copy of these audio tapes was made for each

pastor in Honduras.

The 18 departmento coordinators delivered these tapes to the pastors.

For this job they were called back into the office to be familiarized with the training cassette tape.

Through their reports we determined just how many tapes each coordinator needed to take back to his state.

Once there, the departmento coordinators would begin to travel again to every town and personally deliver this most valuable training tool to every pastor.

During the weeks following this, all the ministry teams were instructed by the Executive Staff to try to fulfill every invitation to meet with churches and pastors.

This constant personal contact was vitally important.

We must keep the excitement and expectation at a high level until the census actually starts.

It would be so easy to allow the momentum to die out just because of inattention.

We believe that to be one of the biggest challenges during this very crucial time period.

Keep the census takers ready and excited by keeping the pastors ready and excited!

For Honduras, we had 500,000 Spanish Living New Testaments (Nuevo Testamento Viviente) printed. This was to be our witness/census-taking tool.

This tool is very unique.

In the front are several very special pages.

One page is a "love letter" from Charles and Frances to the person receiving the Bible.

The next page in the New Testament is the main witnessing tool used by the census taker.

Figure 4a
(Side One)

God loves **you,** and has a wonderful **plan** for your life!

"For God so loved the world, that He gave His only begotten Son, that whoever believes in Him should not perish, but have eternal life." (John 3:16)

Jesus speaking: "I came that they might have life, and might have it abundantly." (John 10:10)

"For all have sinned and fall short of the glory of God." (Romans 3:23)

"For the wages of sin is death." (Romans 6:23)

"But God demonstrates His own love toward us, in that while we were yet sinners, Christ died for us." (Romans 5:8)

Jesus said to him, "I am the way, and the truth, and the life; no one comes to the Father, but through Me." (John 14:6)

"But as many as received Him, to them He gave the right to become children of God, even to those who believe in His name." (John 1:12)

"Behold, I stand at the door and knock; if any one hears My voice and opens the door, I will come in to him." (Revelation 3:20)

This WONDERFUL PLAN lists eight scriptures which are basic to a person receiving Jesus.

The census taker leads the person through those one by one.

Then on the next page of their New Testament there is a very basic prayer which the census-taker can help the person pray.

Figure 4b
(Side Two)

Lord Jesus, I need You. Thank You for dying on the cross for my sins. I open the door to my life and receive You as my Savior and Lord. Thank You for forgiving my sins and giving me eternal life. Take control of the throne of my life. Make me the kind of person You want me to be.

____ / __________
Signature **Date**

I am saved!

For street witnessing and to the homeless, we printed these simple witness tools on a 4-1/4" x 5-1/2" colored paper. The form is folded so side one, the inside, is for the scriptures (WONDERFUL PLAN) and on side two is the prayer and signature; the other side is "I Am Saved!" This makes a small desk sign.

Next is a section giving the spiritually newborn some practical suggestions on what to do next.

Such things as how to read the Bible, pray, and the importance of being filled with the Holy Spirit.

Also included in this section is a page for notes as the new member of the body of Christ begins to commune with the Lord through His word.

One other training item was included with the Bibles. (See Figures 5 and 6). With these a pastor was able to thoroughly train all his people to become very effective census takers and witnesses.

You have no problems which will not be overcome when God tells you to do a work like the Honduras census, but there are daily challenges through which God leads His workers.

Unique challenges were presented in Honduras when it came to getting these materials into the hands of all the pastors.

The Bibles arrived at Puerto Cortez on the northern coast of Honduras.

Using the figures given us by the departmento coordinators, we were able to estimate just how many "sets" of training materials were needed in each district.

(One set consists of one Bible and several census forms. (See census form Figure 7, Page 164). The materials were loaded in trucks at the port and taken to San Pedro Sula, the nearest large town we were using as one of the three distribution points.

There the materials were divided by volunteers into the right amount needed for the other two distribution points, Tegucigalpa and Santa Rosa.

These supplies were then shipped to each of those cities.

INSTRUCTIONS
(Figure 5)

1. You have a map and address or location of each home to which you are assigned to preach the gospel.

2. You have received instructions personally, through audio or video tapes, or otherwise as to the houses you are to touch.

3. Every member in each house is to be contacted, all at once if possible, but if one is not at home, you are to continue returning until you have made contact with every person. Jesus said the gospel will be preached to every person on earth, and that includes each person in homes to which you have been assigned.

4. The census form is to be carefully completed, printing the information clearly.

5. Be very friendly with each person you visit. Do not argue scripture.

6. Once you have completed the census forms with all names in the home and other information requested on the form, return your forms to your leader, normally your pastor, but it may be some individual who is coordinator of the area.

SPIRITUAL INSTRUCTIONS

(Figure 6)

(Honduras received New Testaments; adapt this for cards (Figure 4a and b)

1. Knock on each door in your territory; when a person comes to the door, introduce yourself and state your purpose in being there in a friendly, but clear manner.
   The Christians of your city from all denominations are taking a census of every person in your city. Just as Jesus said it would be done, the gospel will be preached to every person on earth, and then He will return.
2. May I share with you very briefly how this will bless you?
3. Fill in names and address on Census Registration Form first.
4. Then present the gospel as you have been trained. You should use the "Wonderful Plan" by showing them Side One which has every scripture necessary for them to understand the gospel and how to receive Jesus as their Savior. Explain that they are not joining any church, but can continue in the church of their choice.
5. Ask them, "Have you ever asked Jesus to come into your life?"
6. Show them the little prayer on Side Two; read it aloud to them, and then say, "Would you like to pray this prayer with me?"
7. Read a phrase and have them repeat it, until they have said the entire prayer. Then say, "Where is Jesus right now?" They should reply, "In my life," or "In my heart."

8. Tell them you would like to leave this New Testament (or card) with them and ask them each to sign the New Testament (or card) with the date to remember the day they were saved.
9. If you have received the baptism with the Holy Spirit yourself, then ask them if they have ever heard of the baptism with the Holy Spirit and speaking in tongues. If not (or if they say "Yes" but do not resist your offering them this wonderful gift) instruct them briefly as you have been taught, then pray aloud in tongues. Then ask if they would like to receive this great gift from God. If so, minister to them.
10. Ask if anyone in the home needs healing. If so, explain how Jesus anointed us to minister healing and, by the power of God's Holy Spirit, in the name of Jesus Christ, they can be healed. If you have had the video or audio training and read the books HOW TO HEAL THE SICK and HANDBOOK FOR HEALING, you should have great success in ministering healing.
11. Complete the census form.
12. Tell them about the cell group Bible study, where and when it will be held, and invite the whole family to attend. Contact them a day or two before the Bible study to insure their coming. If anyone fails to attend any Bible study, quickly contact them.
13. Your work is complete, but if you choose to later visit with them more, then offer help in any way you can give it to them.

DISTRIBUTION CHART
(Figure No. 8a)

(Nation divided into 3 districts)

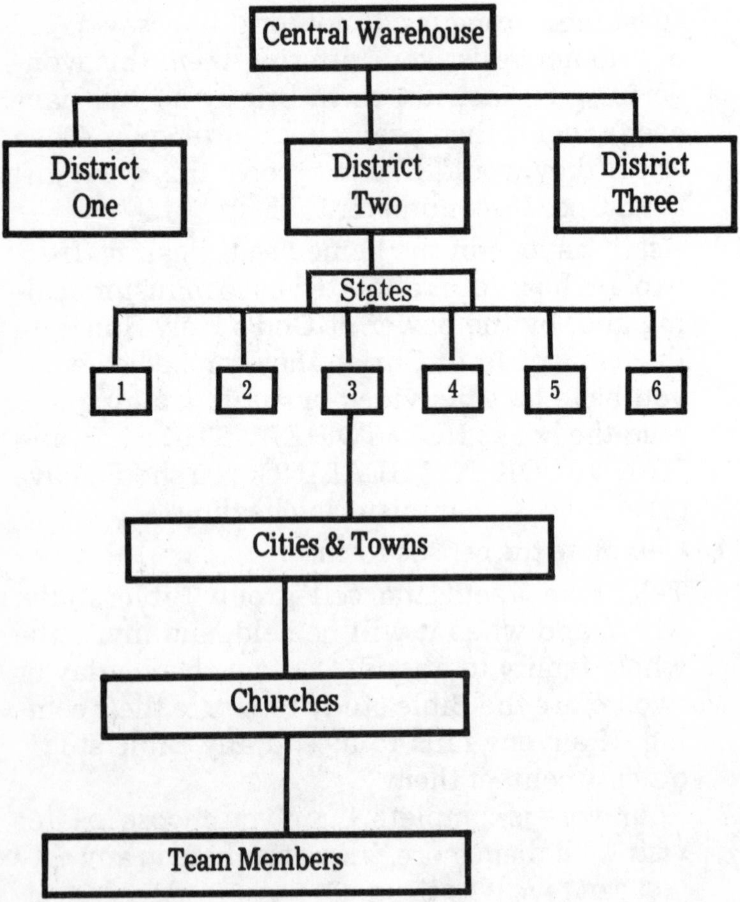

Distribution Chart
(Figure No. 8b)

To get all materials into each team's hands, the following plan was implemented.

We needed to determine how many sets of materials were required for each state, city and town.

The estimated population of each town was determined.

This gave us a close estimate of how many homes are in each town. By finding this figure for each town and adding them all together we could determine how many sets were needed for each state. This figure x 6 states gave us the amount of supplies to be sent to each of the three districts.

1. All materials were shipped into Honduras to a central distribution port.
2. The nation was divided into three districts. Each district is made up of six states. The Bibles and materials were divided into the number of packages needed for each state and shipped from the port to the three district distribution centers by large trucks.
3. The correct number of sets of materials were then shipped by buses to each state coordinator from the district coordinator for each state.

At the state level, the coordinator and his volunteers divided the materials again.

This time into amounts needed for each city, town and village.

4. These amounts were shipped to the assigned coordinating pastor in each city and town.

At this level, we used whatever shipping method was available.

In some cases by bus, in others by truck, personal car, mule, or whatever else we could find, some walking and lovingly, laboriously carrying the census tools on back packs.

5. Once in the hands of the assigned coordinating pastor in each city or town, he had the responsibility to distribute the Bibles and other material to the local pastors of each church in the proper amounts.

As soon as a pastor received his materials and signed a receipt for them, he was asked to start the training of his teams. He was not to give out the Bibles and census materials to the teams until January 5, 1991. When the Bibles and census forms were finally given to the census teams, each was required to sign a receipt for the number of packages given to them, one for each home assigned to the team.

The pastor would have four to six weeks in which to prepare his people to capture the section of town over which he had assumed responsibility.

Because of the simplicity of the training and the "technique" God had given, that would be plenty of time.

This training would continue right up until the time the census was to start.

TAKING THE CENSUS

The day set to start the history-making evangelistic census was Saturday morning, January 5, 1991, the time was 8:00 o'clock.

We scheduled a "count-down" on nation-wide radio for the week before.

At every opportunity we held rallies, meetings, whatever we could do to keep the momentum at a high rate.

Then, at last, the day arrives!

All over the nation the teams are poised and ready.

They know what to do!

They are armed with their Bibles!

They have their census forms!

They know their assigned areas!

And, at precisely 8:00 o'clock they ATTACK!

As each team completes a census form, they keep it in a place where it cannot get misplaced.

Daily they must turn the completed census reports back to their pastor.

From there it will begin its journey back to the national headquarters in Tegucigalpa for the final count!

Each team has been informed during their training that they are to play a very special part in the follow-up.

The follow-up is to be a thirty-six week Bible study that will take place over nation-wide radio. The team is to invite all those on their census route, particularly those they lead to Jesus, to their house or a designated place on one of the two nights on which the follow-up Bible study classes will be aired.

There they will become a very special part of each person's life.

CENSUS REGISTRATION FORM
(Figure 7)

FATHER'S NAME

____

☐ Already Born Again ☐ Accepted Jesus ☐ Did not accept Jesus ☐ Healed

MOTHER'S NAME

____

☐ Already Born Again ☐ Accepted Jesus ☐ Did not accept Jesus ☐ Healed

CHILDREN/AGES:

____

☐ Already Born Again ☐ Accepted Jesus ☐ Did not accept Jesus ☐ Healed

____

☐ Already Born Again ☐ Accepted Jesus ☐ Did not accept Jesus ☐ Healed

____

☐ Already Born Again ☐ Accepted Jesus ☐ Did not accept Jesus ☐ Healed

____

☐ Already Born Again ☐ Accepted Jesus ☐ Did not accept Jesus ☐ Healed

NAME OF ILLNESS HEALED:

____

FAMILY ADDRESS: (Street, Apt. No.)

____

(City, State and Zip)

____

CHURCH RESPONSIBLE: ______________________________

Name

Pastor: ______________________________

Address: ______________________________

____

City **State** **Zip**

Phone (**)** ______________

CENSUS TAKERS:

____

Names Printed

____

SUMMARY OF EVANGELISTIC CENSUS

HONDURAS, CENTRAL AMERICA - JANUARY, 1991

(Figure 8a)

SUMMARY LEVEL	NO. PEOPLE SAVED (Yes)	NOT SAVED (No)	NUMBER PEOPLE HEALED	TOTAL TEAMS	TOTAL CHURCHES	TOTAL CITIES	TOTAL STATES	TOTAL PEOPLE CONTACTED
TEAM								
CHURCH								
CITY								
STATE								
DISTRICT								
NATION								

TEAM: Each TEAM will personally deliver the census forms for all houses contacted, and give the census forms to the pastor or leader in charge of their church (Figure 9a, Page 166).

CHURCH: Each CHURCH will summarize the census forms for all the census teams from their church and send the SUMMARY ONLY to their CITY DIRECTOR (Figure 9b, Page 167). Pastors, keep team reports for follow-up.

CITY: Each CITY DIRECTOR will summarize the census forms for all the churches assigned to him, and send ALL the church sensus summaries plus his CITY summary to his STATE Director.

STATE: Each STATE DIRECTOR will summarize the census forms for the CITIES in his state, and hand carry ALL the CHURCH AND CITIES census forms, along with the STATE summary form, to his DISTRICT DIRECTOR.

DISTRICT: Each DISTRICT DIRECTOR will summarize the census forms for the states in his district, hand carry ALL the CHURCH, CITY, AND STATE census forms, along with his DISTRICT summary form, to the NATIONAL OFFICE.

NATIONAL: The NATIONAL DIRECTOR will summarize the final national census forms for all the three districts to reflect the final results of the evangelistic census for the nation.

SUMMARY CENSUS REPORT
(Figure No. 9a)

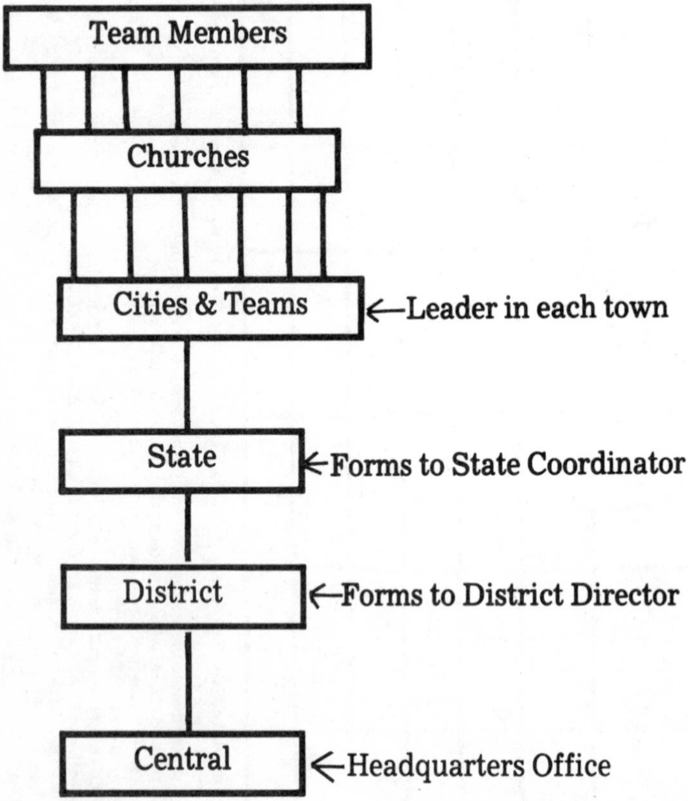

Summary Census Report Forms
(Figure No. 9b)

Team Member: Turns in all completed forms to his pastor.

Pastor: Each pastor tabulates the results of his teams, then turns this information in to the designated coordinator for his city.

City Coordinator: This person receives all the reports from local pastors. Then sends them on to the State Director in the state capitol city.

State Director: The State Director gets all the returned reports and checks the summaries for mistakes. He then forwards the reports to the District Director.

District Director: He gathers all reports and sends them to the home office for final counting.

CENSUS FORMS
(Figure 7)

We made the census form as simple as possible; perhaps you will want to include other information, but still we urge that it be kept very simple.

SUMMARY OF EVANGELISTIC CENSUS FORM
(Figure 8)

The forms and instructions are fully explained in Figure 8 a & b. You will note that when the census is completed we leave all the census forms with the local pastors for follow-up. These should be kept in a permanent file by each pastor, so if further studies by other churches or districts are desired, they can have access to them.

All the SUMMARIES are passed along to the next higher level for analysis and reporting purposes and finally end up in the national headquarters.

From these summaries the announcement is made at the Harvest Celebration concerning how many people have accepted Jesus during the two-week period, as well as how many heard the gospel as Jesus announced.

These will be used as part of the follow-up operation.

The census results are important, but the most important part is for the teams and churches to follow-up on each person contacted, and keep working on the ones who were not available for the census until all have had the gospel preached to every person in the census territory.

WITNESS TOOLS
(Figure 4 a & b)

In Honduras we used a very simple presentation of the gospel, but it has proven most successful.

If you choose to use your own plan of witnessing, that is totally satisfactory.

If you have used something like THE FOUR SPIRITUAL LAWS by Campus Crusade for Christ, the tools by Billy Graham Evangelistic teams, or some other tools, please choose that which you feel the Holy Spirit leads you to use.

We included the witness tools in the front of the Living New Testament we gave to every home in Honduras. For the homeless, we used the forms similar to the brochure reproduced as shown in Figures 4a & b (Pages 154 and 155).

We experienced phenomenal results with this simple presentation of the gospel.

The more simple the presentation, the less training is needed for the witness teams.

In one test village of about 3,000 population, we trained 35 people on Friday night and sent them out for the evangelization of their area at 8:00 o'clock the next morning.

The results were astounding: The few teams we had contacted about 700 people in two or three hours after receiving a little over two hours of training and instructions. Of these 700 contacted, about 500 were saved.

There were two small churches in the village (one having about 25 in attendance; the other about 20).

Sunday morning came after the evangelistic

sample census was completed. The two churches combined their morning service in one church, and the night service in the other.

Attending each service there were over 500, most of whom were new converts from the day before.

We heard from the churches again about two or three weeks later. The attendance in both churches grew so much that people were standing outside. The poor pastors — they are trying to find larger facilities, but there are none in their village. All they can do is hold multi-services on Sunday, Monday, Tuesday, Wednesday, Thursday, Friday, and Saturday!

This sample testing in preparation for the January, 1991 census indicated that over 75% contacted were saved.

We have prepared a brochure for the United States, or any nation, state, city or area, in Chapter 9, entitled, "How To Mobilize and Evangelize a Nation" which is self-explanatory and is presented on Pages 191-198. This brochure may be reproduced or changed to suit your plan, without approval from our ministry.

Study the brochure and see how easy it is for you to gather the pastors and leaders of your area and hold an evangelistic census. Try it in the area around your church and see the marvelous results you will have.

You will discover that an evangelistic census will bring excitement to your church or group or denomination. It will raise the spiritual level to an all-time high, whether it involves a church or a nation.

People often ask us how we stay full of zeal

after over twenty years in ministry. The answer is simple: we daily do what Jesus did daily! Just imagining the joy expressed by the angels in heaven should fill us with more abundant thrills than anything ever experienced on earth. That is our way of life and it can be the normal lifestyle of every born-again believer in the world.

Do you get the feeling that we expect you to do all the same things we are doing, which are the same things done by the early New Testament church? If Charles and Frances can do it, you can do it too, because Jesus said so!

Stage "C" & "D"

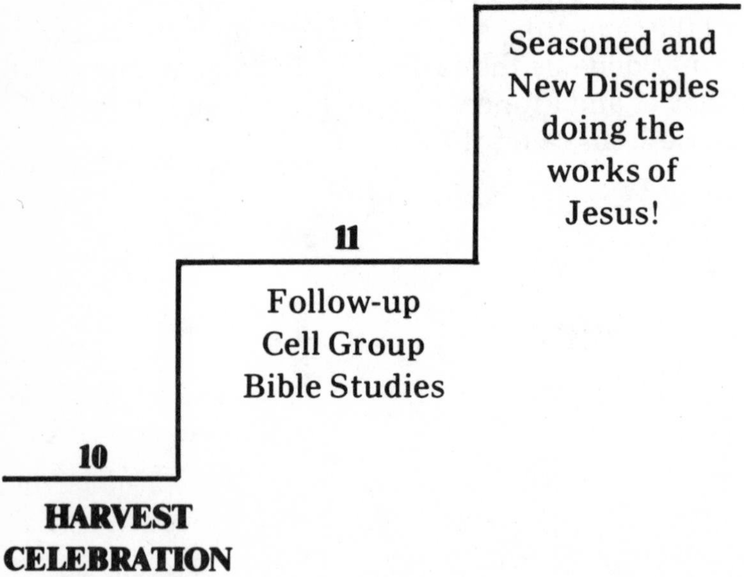
Seasoned and New Disciples doing the works of Jesus!
11
Follow-up Cell Group Bible Studies
10
HARVEST CELEBRATION

Stage "C"

10. The Harvest Celebration is to be a grand night of praise, worship, challenge and commitment. It will offer thanks to God for the souls won during the two weeks of witnessing.

    The coordinator in each area (state) will come into the arena with a flaming torch and proclaim how many people have accepted Jesus in his departmento (state). Testimonies of accomplishments for Jesus will be given. A great Healing Explosion by the trained healing teams will conclude the Harvest Celebration.

Stage "D"

11. The follow-up will be designed to "make disciples" of those who have been saved.

    In Honduras it is conducted on nation-wide radio. Two sessions per week are aired. Plus a 30 minute special program for the cell leaders.

    In that program, the cell leader is advised what the next lesson will be and is encouraged to make contact with all those in his group and remind them of the meeting.

    The sessions will last for possibly thirty-six weeks and include basic Christian living, walking in the Holy Spirit, signs and wonders, witnessing and much, much more!

This is the way we envision the climax of the Honduras Evangelistic Census and Harvest Celebration:

The great day of the giant *Harvest Celebration* in the capitol city, Tegucigalpa, has arrived. This is a time of praise, worship, sharing, and reporting to the nation the results of the *Evangelistic Census*. . . .

The celebration begins at 2:00 p.m. with a parade of all choirs of all churches, marching through streets singing victory praise to God.

Thousands of believers on foot will be moving as a giant army returning from a great victory! They sing and worship as they march toward the plaza.

They are already rejoicing over the 2,000,000 souls who have come into God's kingdom during the two weeks' period. They are led by the Honduran Army Band.

Soon they arrive at the plaza.

In quick order the seats are all full.

Then they begin to fill the side streets for blocks.

No traffic can move.

The air is electric with excitement and expectation.

Inside and just behind the giant platform, a 100 voice choir begins to sing.

The praise fills the air as the huge crowd begins to catch the spirit of celebrating a great move of God, and they join the praise.

The guests on the stage begin to praise and the involvement of the entire crowd swells.

After a time of praise, the master of ceremonies steps to the mike.

He introduces the mayor of Tegucigalpa. The

mayor welcomes everyone. Then the Army Band strikes up the Honduran national anthem, after which the color guard presents the colors!

The mayor, visibly moved with emotion, expresses her gratitude and expectation at what this is going to do in her country — spiritually, economically and socially.

With that, the Harvest Celebration Band begins a rousing praise session.

Other important people are introduced.

Charles and Frances then thank the Honduran people for their cooperation and congratulate them on successfully completing this history-making work of God.

Then, a moment of silence.

Suddenly the sound of a drum march bursts over the 36 speakers located throughout the plaza and echoes down the streets.

Then the sounds of a full orchestra break forth. The 100 voice choir begins to sing "PROCLAIM HIM KING."

The choir continues the proclamation with "SHOUT! FOR GOD HAS GIVEN US HONDURAS."

Then as suddenly as it began, the mood changes.

The music becomes soft.

The choir begins to worship with "Hallelujah", sung just above a whisper.

Charles steps to the mike. "Will the torch bearer from Olancho enter!"

From the far side of the plaza a lone figure comes running!

Overhead he carries a flaming torch!

On he runs until he stops in front of the torch stand!

Into the mike which stands there he shouts, *"The state of Olancho brings 38,000 to Jesus!"*

The crowd shouts!

The intensity of the music and the choir increases slightly.

Frances calls for another torch bearer.

Another runner!

Another torch!

"The state of Valle brings 51,000 to Jesus!"

Still another runner.

Then another.

Until 18 have arrived at the torch stand, made their announcement, and placed their torch into the stand. When all 18 torches have been placed in the holder, it will not appear as 18 different lights, but as one huge light indicating that all of Honduras has seen the great light of Jesus!

God said, "Take a census of the world" and Honduras would be the first nation where the gospel would be preached to every creature. *History will have been made in Honduras!*

Now the music starts softly.

The choir joins the music with words. "Mine eyes have seen the glory of the coming of the Lord...." The song builds...and builds...and builds...until it seems that the very angels of heaven have joined in.

The closing refrain is a mighty sound of both orchestra and voices.

The crowd is wild with praise now. The choir is seated on or near the platform. As the song ends, five foot high letters held by ten Hondurans are illuminated by candles burning with a bright flame. The message they tell has only one word — JESUS!

Then Charles and Frances will lead the audience in a victory and salvation prayer.

Just before ministering the baptism with the Holy Spirit, they will announce that they are going to minister the baptism and follow that with a great Healing Explosion. "Healing teams, be ready to do great signs and wonders in ministering healing to this vast audience who came believing, expecting and obeying Jesus."

Then Frances will make the call for the baptism with the Holy Spirit, and Charles will minister from the stage. We are believing God for 80% of the audience to receive this great and mighty gift from God.

Typical of all the Healing Explosions around the world, and particularly in the Spanish speaking world, the healing teams will see the greatest healings ever seen in Honduras.

And Jesus said, *"And these signs will follow those who believe: In My name they will cast out demons; they will speak with new tongues; they will take up serpents; and if they drink anything deadly, it will by no means hurt them; they will lay hands on the sick, and they will recover"* (Mark 16:17,18).

The last words Jesus spoke on earth and which have echoed throughout the ages will have been completed in HONDURAS!

At some point in the service, the nation-wide water baptism service will be announced for all who desire to enter into this covenant with Jesus. We are believing God that more than one million people will be baptized in water as all who desire to participate will hold simultaneous water baptism services throughout the land. We will conduct a water baptismal service in a local facility, broadcasting on nation-wide radio. This will let all of the nation have an opportunity to share in the ordinance and receive instructions and inspiration as they join in every area of Honduras.

Then like the might of 10,000 angels, the trained healing teams identified by a small red ribbon will go into action and minister healing to all who have come believing for a miracle. They won't quit until all have received ministry.

The whole world is about to take notice of what God has planned for this final decade of harvest in preparation for the return of Jesus!

God said, "Honduras will be the first nation on earth where the gospel will be preached to every creature."

It is finished!

Chapter 9

Let's Bring This To The U.S.A.

After realizing what will happen in the third world countries, including the model nation Honduras, our first and immediate response was, "This will never work in the United States."

Then we said, "Why not?"

If we believe that with God all things are possible, then how can we say it cannot work in the United States?

Can we say that God cannot unite all of the separate denominations for a common purpose of saving the lost?

Can we say that God is not big enough to bring unity to those people who have come so vehemently against tongues, or even the Pentecostal denominations which come so vehemently against one another, or those who speak in tongues belittling those who don't?

God's word in Ephesians 4:11 declares that we will have unity in the body of Christ — and the time for this is very near!

In Winston-Salem, North Carolina, we met

with two pastors in the area and shared with them the vision that we're sharing in this book.

As we talked about Central America and broadcasting over one radio station, a daring thought entered our minds!

Why couldn't that happen in the United States?

Why couldn't we have all of the Christian television and radio networks across the nation, who are all competing for the same Christian dollar, and competing for the same Christian audience, cooperate for one hour during one day each week for a single nondenominational Bible study and a second hour for a follow-up program?

Can you anticipate in your wildest imagination what would happen if we could get to that point where TBN would cooperate with CBN who would cooperate with Lester Sumrall who would cooperate with Russ Bixler who would cooperate with Morris Cerullo, who would cooperate with Jerry Falwell, and so forth and so on down the line, from the biggest stations to the smallest stations?

Could we somehow or another, because of the love of God within our hearts, join together and have one hour a day across the United States with everyone broadcasting exactly the same thing — precisely what's happening in Honduras?

Would we be so involved in fighting that every network would want their own stars teaching?

These are questions that must be answered deep within our hearts by asking, "Is this what God is saying today?"

Is God telling the body of Christ to unite totally and completely and not worry about who gets the glory and who gets the money, and not worry about who is going to build their ministry the most?

As far as we are concerned, we don't want any glory, we don't want our ministry to be a huge ministry, all we want to do is to see the work of Jesus completed!

It will never be completed until we are willing to lay down all of these things which have separated us for so many years!

That, of course, doesn't mean that all of the television and radio programs would have to stop their work; it would simply mean that they are united for the single purpose that Jesus is saying will be done before He comes back — that every creature on earth will hear the gospel.

It can be done very simply in the United States and we think it would increase the listening audience of the various television and radio stations.

It would bring a unity where more people would watch these programs until they would become a great boost to every television and every radio station in the country.

If every cell group Bible study took up an offering during the television or radio lesson and discussion and sent it to the station broadcasting to them, surely the stations would be amply and equitably financed.

Is this chapter an imaginary thing or can it become a reality?

We believe it's a reality because as we have shared the concept that we have shared in this book, we have seen pastors go out and start winning their cities to Jesus.

We are seeing in different states pastors catching the vision and saying, "Yes, we will go with it."

In talking to pastors, we have discovered the most difficult thing in the world is to get a group of pastors together for a meeting for the benefit of their particular city.

A letter sent out brings very little response.

How are we going to overcome these years of prejudice and these years of selfishness and these years of tradition that "my denomination can't work with yours," "my station can't work with yours," "we can't cooperate with each other."

We can see across the United States one hour in the morning and one hour at night of a united body of Christ on every television and radio station in our nation for one purpose.

Can you imagine the impact upon salvation if we did this?

Can you imagine the impact, if say, some 20,000,000 to 50,000,000 people in the United States were trained to go out and win people to Jesus?

Then at a signal given on satellite and via radio and television, these trained witness teams, like census takers, went out like a bunch of locusts going across the United States on the same day to eat up and to devour what the devil has done to this great land of ours.

We read a statement in a book recently which said, "All great discoveries have been made by people whose faith ran ahead of their minds."

We'd like to say, "No great accomplishment has ever been made in the kingdom of God except by people whose faith ran ahead of their minds."

In the natural mind there is no way that this could ever be possible and yet in the supernatural power of God and in the supernatural working of God, this is totally and completely possible and what we feel God wants the entire body of Christ to do.

We have tried to evangelize our world with mass crusades, and yet if we would very simply read the Bible it tells us exactly how they covered all of Asia Minor in two years.

What's going to happen if you get opposition?

You can rest assured that there is going to be opposition because no one in the Bible ever started doing something for God without ending up in great big trouble and without receiving all kinds of opposition.

Exactly the same thing happens today, so when you get a vision of what God is telling you to do, you have to go on with it whether anybody else agrees with you or not.

Maybe you would be the only person in your town who catches a vision from God, but if you're that person, run with it and don't pay any attention to the opposition coming your way.

When God spoke to us and said, "Take a census of the world" that was too big for any single individual or all of us Christians combined to comprehend or believe possible, except it's not too big for God.

When God said Honduras would be the first nation on earth where the gospel would be preached to every creature, we had faith without a doubt and obeyed Him instantly, because we heard Him say so!

When we arrived in Honduras, there was opposition, there were impossible situations, some said it couldn't be done; but by the time you read this book *it will have been done.*

We can look at the negative side and say nothing can be done, but God says in Matthew 19:26, *But Jesus looked at them and said to them, With men this is impossible, but with God all things are possible.*

We must not look at what has or has not been done in the past, but realize God and Christ Jesus mean what they say.

Recently we heard several people make comments as to what they thought would happen during this last decade, what's going to be happening in the next year or two.

All kinds of answers came back, including those who said, "We're going to have a stronger power of the devil. We're going to have to spend more time in spiritual warfare!"

What Jesus said was that we're going to end up with a victorious church, a mighty church, a glorious church.

As we enter this final phase of the works of Jesus, we're sure the devil is shuddering.

Remember what we said, "Not since the resurrection of Jesus have there been such shock waves ringing through hell as there have been since God said, 'Take a census of the world.'"

The best weapon for spiritual warfare is *light!*

Jesus is the light of the world. Light simply makes darkness disappear. When God said, "Let there be light," light came and darkness vanished.

Jesus said, *"You are the light of the world"* (Matthew 5:14) — just as He was the light of the world. He is living His life in us and through us and that same light of God will shine forth through us if we're doing what Jesus said.

Every time we go out to preach the gospel, every time somebody receives salvation, the baptism, healing, deliverance or freedom from the bonds of the devil, our light shines.

A lot is being said and done about "spiritual warfare" today, and a lot of excitement and emotion has been generated among the body of Christ concerning this particular doctrine.

Like a lot of doctrinal "off-shoots", things can become unbalanced without keeping the proper emphasis on the ENTIRE Great Commission.

You can become overbalanced on healing, and do nothing else!

You can become overbalanced on prayer, and do nothing else!

You can become overbalanced on casting out devils, and do nothing else!

You can become overbalanced on discipleship, and do nothing else!

You can become overbalanced on the gifts of the Spirit, and do nothing else!

You can become overbalanced on prophecy, and do nothing else!

All of these things are good, providing they point to the reason Jesus came to earth and left it in the hands of his disciples — to fulfill the Great Commission as it appears in Matthew 28:18-20 and Mark 16:15-20.

What did Jesus do about "spiritual warfare?"

The Amplified Translation beautifully explains exactly how Jesus handled the devil himself, and we should do the same likewise.

Luke 4:1-14 says, *Then Jesus, full of and controlled by the Holy Spirit, returned from the Jordan, and was led in (by) the (Holy) Spirit*

For (during) forty days in the wilderness (desert), where He was tempted (tried, tested exceedingly) by the devil. And He ate nothing during those days, and when they were completed, He was hungry.

Then the devil said to Him, If You are the Son of God, order this stone to turn into a loaf [of bread].

And Jesus replied to him, It is written, Man shall not live and be sustained by (on) bread alone but by every word and expression of God.

Then the devil took Him up to a high mountain and showed Him all the kingdoms of the habitable world in a moment of time — in the twinkling of an eye.

And he said to Him, To You I will give all this power and authority and their glory (that is, all their magnificence, excellence, preeminence, dignity and grace,) for it has been turned over to me, and I give it to whom I will;

Therefore if You will do homage to and worship me (just once), it shall all be Yours.

And Jesus replied to him, Get behind Me, Satan! It is written, You shall do homage to and worship the Lord your God, and Him only shall you serve.

Then he took Him to Jerusalem and set Him on a gable of the temple, and said to Him, If You are the Son of God, cast Yourself down from here;

For it is written, He will give His angels charge of you to guard and watch over you closely and carefully;

And on their hands they will bear you up, lest you strike your foot against a stone.

And Jesus replied to him, [The Scripture] says, You shall not tempt (try, test exceedingly) the Lord your God.

And when the devil had ended every [the complete cycle of] temptation, he left Him — temporarily, that is, stood off from Him until another more opportune and favorable time.

Then Jesus went back full of and under the power of the (Holy) Spirit into Galilee, and the fame of Him spread through the whole region round about.

Jesus KNEW who He was, and He stood firm on what He knew and believed!

He spoke the Word and the devil was defeated!

The scripture tells us in James 4:7, "*Therefore submit to God, Resist the devil and he will flee from you.*"

God is not a God on the defensive, He is a God on the offensive!

If you "submit to God", preach the Good News and lead people to Jesus, you have defeated the devil and he will flee from you!

The word "submit" has many meanings, some of which are "yield, comply, obey, defer to, be subject to, capitulate, surrender" and many others very similar in nature.

Whichever way you look at it, it means very simply to obey what God tells you to do.

Capitulate and surrender your will and do what the Bible tells us to do!

Recently a group of Christians were discussing spiritual warfare, and one of them said: "Someone gets an idea which sounds good, and expands it to make an entire doctrine out of it. Then because the body of Christ is always looking for something new and different, it begins to spread, and before long, everyone is getting away from the purpose for which Jesus came to earth — to save the lost!"

When we come home at night, the house is dark!

We do not come sneaking in the door with our machete knives slashing through the air!

We do not come in the door screaming and yelling for that darkness to disappear!

We do not stand at the front door and command that devil of darkness to come out of our house!

We do not stand at our front door and pray in tongues for the darkness to disappear!

Do you know what we do?

We turn the light switch on and the darkness disappears!

Nothing in the world will dispel darkness except light!

Jesus is the light of the world, and He said that we also were the light of the world!

We have been in many hotels, having been in the ministry for over twenty years, and we have never yet stood outside our room and yelled for the darkness to disappear!

We just open the door, flip the light switch, and the darkness is gone!

We believe that although spiritual warfare is real and has many facets, yet the real final spiritual warfare is when we turn on the light by doing the works of Jesus.

The devil can't stand light and his demons scatter like cockroaches when we turn on our light.

We know that's the tool Jesus used.

We find very little fighting the devil in the ministry of Jesus or the disciples who followed Him.

We found that they were out sharing the light of the world until the gospel was preached to every person in all of the then known world in two years.

There were no airplanes, there were no televisions, there were no radios, there were no cars, there was no communication where they could reach out like we can, there was no written Bible except the scripts of the Old Testament which were not readily available to the average person.

But the body of Christ was unified for a single purpose when Peter, James, John and all the other disciples did what Jesus said.

It was fresh on their mind and they went out door-by-door and actually did preach the gospel to every creature!

They tried mass evangelism and that's not wrong.

That will continue until Jesus comes back.

Missionaries won't cease because they're doing a tremendous job.

When all of us join together with that one focal point, that one aim, one purpose, the purpose for which Jesus came to earth, to save the lost and to make them into disciples who will go win others to Jesus, then we're going to see the glory of God!

This church will be a glorious church and we believe it's going to happen this decade!

We believe it's going to happen when the unity of the ministries and the unity of the people come forth to preach the gospel to every creature on earth.

It will happen because Jesus said so.

He gave us the formula.

He gave us the model.

He made it so simple that a child could understand it.

Will we join together?

Will we simply say, "Yes, Jesus will be back soon and we've got to get this job done fast."

We have got to do it like Jesus said.

Can we really preach the gospel to every creature in America?

Can some 260,000,000 people hear the gospel in two weeks?

Impossible!

Yes, in the natural mind it's impossible but when we do it like Jesus said, it's very easy and can be done in two weeks after the organization and preparation of a unified army of God's believers.

The most evangelized square foot of ground in the entire United States is the average church!

Let's get out of the church and into the fields which are white unto harvest! Then the church organization can mature and equip the saints for the work of ministry.

Might we not take some ideas from the Mormons and the Jehovah Witnesses who are rising up so rapidly, and learn to teach our people how to go out and be real soul winners?

Not only that, but to give them a desire to carry in them the very heartbeat of the Lord Jesus Christ — His heartbeat is souls, souls, souls, souls, souls!

You might say, "How do I start?"

Here is a simplified plan for the United States which will work!

HOW TO MOBILIZE AND EVANGELIZE A NATION

Training is one of the key words in making an evangelistic census!

Everyone participating needs to be trained the same way so there will be unity among the believers.

Everyone needs to know how to present Jesus and how to "close the sale!"

The "Plan"

For a city, state or nation, it is exactly the same!

1. Call a meeting of the pastors of all denominations who have a hunger for souls.
2. Share the vision for evangelizing everyone in your city, state or nation.
3. Get volunteers for the Steering Committee to put the "mechanics" together.
4. Get detailed maps of your city, state or nation. These are available through the post offices or government.
5. Mark off large sections of town or towns.
6. Then mark off smaller sections in each large section. (Approximately 35-50 homes per census taker team in each section).
7. Give large maps to cooperating pastors or head of regions, along with smaller maps for them to give out.
8. Have each pastor who has "caught" the vision conduct a meeting in his area looking for volunteers to take care of the logistics for the smaller areas. Every person involved

must have a revelation of the vision!

9. Have head of census provide training for the supporting pastors or representatives on how to teach the people under them.
10. All pastors present vision for evangelization to their church members, then train those interested in HOW TO GIVE A TESTIMONY, HOW TO GO DOOR-TO-DOOR, and PREPARING TO GO DOOR-TO-DOOR.
11. Teach everyone involved how to use summary census form to be returned to pastor for summarization of entire territory assigned to them.
12. Have a Harvest Celebration and Healing Explosion at the conclusion of the evangelistic census!

HOW TO GO DOOR-TO-DOOR

1. Teams should go out in two's, one to talk, and one to pray silently (or add to the conversation if the Holy Spirit tells them to!) "*And He called the twelve to Him, and began to send them out two by two, and gave them power over unclean spirits.*" (Mark 6:7).
2. Knock on the door, ring doorbell or catch someone outside, if possible.
3. Introduce yourself. "Hello, my name is________ I am with the____________ Evangelistic Census and we are visiting your neighborhood today. Could you give me about three minutes to answer some questions?"
4. If person says, "Yes", which they most likely will because you are only asking for such a short period of time, they will ask you inside or keep you on the steps. Either way is satisfactory.

5. Be very friendly and courteous to everyone. Remember you are a representative of the Lord JESUS.
6. Never argue scriptures.
7. Take out CENSUS REGISTRATION FORM.
8. Write down the address from the number on the mailbox or house.
9. Ask for their name, and how many in family.
10. Ask what church they attend, if any.
11. Tell them the Christians in their city from all denominations are taking an evangelistic census of every person. Just as Jesus said it would be done: the gospel will be preached to every person on earth, and then He will return.
12. Ask them, "Have you ever asked Jesus to come into your life (your heart)?" (Whichever you prefer). You might ask them, "Has anyone ever explained to you how to have peace with God?"
13. If they say, "No," read the WONDERFUL PLAN:

GOD HAS A WONDERFUL PLAN
FOR YOUR LIFE!

"*For God so loved the world, that He gave His only begotten Son, that whoever believes in Him should not perish, but have everlasting life*" (John 3:16).

"*The thief does not come except to steal, and to kill, and to destroy. I have come that they may have life, and that they may have it more abundantly*" (John 10:10).

"*For all have sinned and fall short of the glory of God*" (Romans 3:23).

"*For the wages of sin is death*" (Romans 6:23).

> *"But God demonstrates His own love toward us, in that while we were yet sinners, Christ died for us"* (Romans 5:8).
> *"Jesus said to him, 'I am the way, and the truth, and the life; no one comes to the Father, but through Me'"* (John 14:6).
> *"But as many as received Him, to them He gave the right to become the children of God, even to those who believe on His name"* (John 1:12).
> *"Behold, I stand at the door and knock; if any one hears My voice and opens the door, I will come in to him"* (Revelation 3:20).

Make sure you have read this through sufficiently so that you don't stumble. Have them look at it with you.

14. Ask them if they would like to invite Jesus into their heart. If they say, "Yes," have them read the prayer with you on the reverse side of the card.
15. Have them sign the card and then give it to them as a reminder of the occasion.
16. Invite them to the church in the neighborhood: Invite them to the Harvest Celebration (leave flier).
    Have a list of participating area churches.
    Invite them to your church.
    Tell them, "Someone will call you."
17. Thank them, and ask them where Jesus is right now. If they reply, "In my heart," or "In my life," you know they have received salvation.
18. Tell them that their life will never be the same again.
19. Leave booklet with them concerning salvation.

20. When you ask them if they have ever invited Jesus to come into their lives, and they say, "Yes," congratulate them and ask them if they would like to say the prayer again just to rededicate their life.
21. If they say, "No, I'm not interested either," thank them for their time and go on to next house.
22. As the Holy Spirit leads, you might give them a little portion of your personal testimony before you leave.
23. Again, thank them, and ask if you can leave booklet with them.
24. Repeat process at next house.

THINGS TO REMEMBER

Be attentive to their needs.

Everyone responds when they find that you have a genuine interest in them.

Listen to what they are saying, especially if there is any indication of problems in their life.

PREPARING FOR DOOR-TO-DOOR

1. Make sure that you are well groomed.
2. No bad breath, no lack of deodorant and no dirty clothes.
3. Let their first impression of you be such a good one that they will not hesitate to invite you into their home.
4. Wear comfortable shoes so your feet do not hurt!
5. Have all your materials ready so you don't have to fumble around. Know how to use each piece of literature you have.

6. Smile, smile, smile!
7. Be prayed up — don't wait until you get there to do your praying!
8. Don't overdress so that people will look at your clothes instead of your purpose.
9. Be conservative, but attractive in your dress.
10. Normally, women should go with women, and men with men. If you feel that three are better than two, do not hesitate to have two of one sex and one of the other. A married couple is ideal.

HOW TO GIVE A TESTIMONY

"And they overcame him by the blood of the Lamb and by the word of their testimony" (Revelation 12:11).

Your personal testimony can win more people to Jesus than any other tool you can think of! However, one of the most important things to learn is *how* to give a testimony!

There are three points to remember in sharing what happened to you:

1. Before (what you were before salvation)
2. During (what brought about your salvation)
3. After (what God has done in your life)

Our testimony should be such an integral part of our lives that we can give a real "quickie," or as long and with as many details as necessary!

Neither of us ever talk without giving a part of our testimony somewhere in the teaching or exhorting, so be instant in season and out of season with something of your personal testimony which will communicate to the person to whom you are talking.

Never memorize a testimony because when it becomes "rote" it loses its punch.

Change your wording so that you have to "think" about what you are saying!

It will always be similar, but should never be shared exactly the same over and over again.

Pick what part of your testimony will apply to the situation at hand.

If the person is a smoker, tell him how you were delivered from cigarettes!

If a person is an alcoholic, tell him how you were delivered from alcohol!

If a person is on drugs, tell him how you were delivered from drugs. (Obviously, if you never smoked, were never on drugs or alcohol, you can't do that, but pick something that will relate to their present situation)!

Don't exaggerate! Be accurate! Make your testimony short, to the point and exciting!

A testimony may include many things besides your salvation.

You can give a testimony of how God healed you!

A testimony may include how God has prospered you.

Be specific. Don't just say, "God has really blessed me!" Tell something specific He has done for you!

Do not stretch your testimony! Some people "milk" a testimony and could have said the same thing with more punch in a third of the time taken!

Also, do not cut it so short that it has no impact!

Be enthusiastic when you tell what God has done in your life.

An unenthusiastic witness is worthless!

Share someone else's testimony which appealed to you! It's always better to give your own, but many times we give short pieces of someone else's testimony because it fits the occasion!

Tell how God healed your marriage, or possibly used *you* to get someone else's marriage healed!

Don't be "religious" or use Christian cliches when you give your testimony! Tell it like it is (or was)! Don't whitewash yourself in the "before" testimony, and also don't roll in the mud more than you actually did!

Use common sense as to the length of your testimony when you are sharing with someone. They might be in a hurry, and if you make it too long, you will lose them!

Convince yourself that you would accept Jesus from what you just said if you were not saved!

Always CLOSE THE SALE! (Have them pray the "Sinner's Prayer.")

Chapter 10

Three Reasons To Expect Success in Soul Winning

"The day I got saved Jesus opened my mouth, and I haven't shut it since! How anyone can keep bottled up within themselves what Jesus has done for them is beyond my wildest imagination. You cannot fail as a soul winner if you love Jesus!"

I don't always have time to read all the mail that comes our way, but there are some I always read because I KNOW the content is going to be good.

Recently an article which appeared in the Living Word Ministries magazine caught my eye, and they have given me permission to reprint it so that you can be blessed!

This is the year when everyone is talking about the return of Jesus, and the need for witnessing, so this will help you tremendously to get over any hang-ups you have on this subject.

Danny Malady says:

God doesn't call us to do anything that can't be

done.

God is not stupid.

He's God.

When He calls, He equips.

And God has called you to a ministry.

In fact, as soon as all believers are born again, they have an instant ministry called the ministry of reconciliation, that is, to go out in the world and win souls to Christ.

God has given us everything we need to get the job done.

He's given us the truth of His Word, the authority of His name, and the power of His Spirit.

The bottom line is that these are the three reasons we can be successful soul winners.

Let me go further in defining these three reasons for you.

First, we have the Word of God that does not return void (Isa. 55:11).

Whenever you speak the Word, it has an impact.

Hebrews 4:12 (Amplified) says, "for the Word that God speaks is alive and full of power — making it active, operative, energizing and effective; it is sharper than any two-edged sword, penetrating to the dividing line of the breath of life (soul) and (the immortal) spirit, and of joints and marrow (that is, of the deepest parts of our nature) exposing and judging the very thoughts and purposes of the heart."

When you speak the Word it goes right where it's supposed to go — to the person's heart.

The Word will locate and speak to the person right where he is.

When Peter preached the Word in Acts Chapter 2 on the day of Pentecost it says the people were pricked in their hearts.

They were convicted by the Holy Spirit as the Word was preached.

The Word had an immediate impact on their lives and three thousand of them were saved.

The Word didn't come back void.

God hastened to perform His Word, He made it come to pass.

Jeremiah 1:12 (Amplified) says "I am alert and active watching over my Word to perform it."

To be an effective witness, you must learn to place absolute confidence in the integrity of God's Word.

When God says something, He means what He says.

When He says He will do something it will be done (Isa. 46:11, Ezk. 12:25).

God is not a liar.

When we plant the seed of God's Word in the hearts of people it does what it is supposed to do and a process begins.

First the blade, after that the ear, after that the full corn in the ear (Mark 4:26-28).

But if we don't sow that first seed there will never be a harvest.

When you speak the Word of God in witnessing you're doing at least one of three things: 1.) Sowing seed; 2.) Adding to what is already there (watering); 3.) Harvesting. As stated in I Cor. 3:6, "...Paul planted, Apollos watered, God gave the increase."

Let me illustrate this from my life. I came from a denominational background.

I had heard about Jesus but never about the new birth.

The first time I heard however, a seed was sown in my heart.

From the first time until the time I finally received Jesus as my Lord and Savior, God sent a number of people to water that seed.

And, after 10 years, I got the picture.

But it didn't happen the first time I heard and it didn't happen the second time.

But, it finally happened!

God's Word didn't come back void.

In fact, none of those people who witnessed to me were even there when I got saved.

I got saved sitting in the front seat of my car with my wife.

Some people feel that if the person doesn't pray the prayer of faith on the spot when they are witnessing, that they have failed.

This idea is completely false! It is quite the contrary.

Here's the reason why.

When the Word went forth, a seed was planted or watered and that is a victory.

The person you have spoken to is all the more close to receiving Jesus.

Even when a person is an old stone face from start to finish, don't walk away looking like a droopy hound saying, "it didn't work."

Don't dig up the seed you've just planted.

Say, "Bless God I'm going to see that one in heaven because the Word doesn't come back void."

God's Word is truth (John 17:17).

The second reason we can expect success is that

we the believers have been given the right to use the name of Jesus.

Mark 16:17-18 talks about the signs that will follow believers.

These signs are brought about through the authority of Jesus' name and through faith in that name.

Signs and wonders done in Jesus' name will draw attention to Jesus and people will see that God is alive, His power is real and Christianity isn't just a lot of talk.

In Acts 8:5 it says that Philip "went down to the city of Samaria, and preached Christ unto them. And the people with one accord gave heed unto those things which Philip spake, hearing and seeing the miracles which he did" (verse 6).

An effective witness is one who can back up what he has to say with miraculous proof.

We've got the Word and its power to back us up.

The third reason we can expect success in soul winning is because God has given us the power to be successful soul winners. We have the Holy Ghost. Acts 1:8 (Amplified) states, "But you shall receive power—ability, efficiency and might—when the Holy Spirit has come upon you; and you shall be my witnesses in Jerusalem and all Judea and Samaria and to the ends—the very bounds—of the earth."

The word "power" in this verse is translated from the Greek word "dunamis" which means ability, efficiency and might.

In 2 Cor. 3:5 it says our sufficiency is of God not ourselves.

It's the power of God in us, the mighty Holy

Spirit, who empowers us to be witnesses.

We as believers need to place our trust in Him.

All I've said can be simply summarized.

Get your eyes off yourself and your natural ability.

Put them on God and His supernatural ability to make you an effective witness.

Brothers and sisters, God has given us all the equipment we need to get the job of evangelizing the world done.

I know that as you step out in faith and are obedient to God's Word, you'll find that witnessing isn't a hard thing to do.

It is simply yielding to the power of God in you and allowing Him to flow through you to reach the world for Jesus.

So come on, let's DO IT!

Let's go!

Chapter 11

A Mandate From God!

A mandate from God is an irrevocable "order from headquarters" which must be fulfilled by the person to whom it is given, or by others to whom the mandate is applicable!

A mandate from God is a precious trust which God places in certain individuals at certain times for certain of His purposes to fulfill!

A mandate is a privilege to execute because not everyone receives a specific mandate from God during their lifetime, so to those whom God has given a mandate, we must do all we can to see that it is carried out!

A mandate from God is a priceless honor to be placed in your hands by the Almighty God!

God spoke to us in Minneapolis, Minnesota on a Saturday afternoon in December of 1985 and said, "Put your video healing tapes in the languages of the world!"

It was not a choice — it was a command from God!

We were temporarily stunned because of the

size of the job!

Realizing the magnanimity of this mandate, the costs involved and the work involved, I said, "God, how come you chose two such old people as we are to do this big job?"

We were 138 years old together at the time.

God's answer was so simple, there could never be any misunderstanding of what He meant.

He merely said, "Because you two are dumb enough to do what I tell you to do!"

I quickly thought back over our lives as Christians, and realized that whatever God has told us to do, we have done to the very best of our ability without ever questioning God!

I thought about the day I got saved when God said, "I want 20% of everything you've got!"

I never questioned Him.

I just obeyed!

I thought about the time God told me to give away my printing business in which I had shed blood, sweat and tears to make it a success!

I never questioned Him.

I just did it!

When God spoke to Charles and to me and told us we were to be married, even though we had never had a date, we never questioned Him!

Even though we missed each other in the airport when Charles came to claim me as his bride, because we barely knew what each other looked like, we never questioned God.

We just did it!

We celebrated our 21st perfect wedding anniversary on January 1, 1991 without ever having an argument, a fight, or a cross word with each other because Jesus is the center of our lives, our home and our marriage!

I remember the morning God spoke to Charles and said, "Teach the people that if you can heal the sick, so can they!"

We never questioned God!

We just did it!

And today, the motto of our ministry is, "If Charles and Frances can do it, you can do it, too!"

We are two ordinary people who now total 144 years, who are just simple enough in their love of and trust in God to follow His instructions without questioning them!

We were obedient, and began immediately to make arrangements for lip syncing and overdubbing our video healing tapes in foreign languages!

Today, it is possible for 80% of the world's population to hear the fourteen hour video healing tapes in their own native language and read the book in their native tongues!

An impossible task, and yet a task that has been accomplished and is still being accomplished!

Only God could do this, but people in virtually every nation on earth are now daily ministering healing as a lifestyle because of these tools.

We realize now that this HOW TO HEAL THE SICK training was a forerunner of the great world-census evangelism!

When God gave us a mandate to take the Great Commission, including healing, around the world, we did not take it lightly, but have consistently forged ahead to get the job completed!

On March 31, 1990, God gave us another mandate.

He spoke very simply to Charles, during a morning meeting in Austin, Texas.

He said only six words, "Take a census of the world!"

What an awe-inspiring mandate!

It was not spoken to us to accomplish by ourselves, it was spoken to the entire body of Christ but was given to us to proclaim to all nations.

God said, "What you do, do quickly!"

On May 29, 1990, God spoke to Frances and said, "Honduras will be the first nation in the world where the census will be taken!"

At the time we received each of these mandates, we were involved in other work, and yet we heard the voice of God.

God did not say, "Let's try doing it like a census." He merely said, "Take a census of the world!"

God did not say, "Why don't you try it in Honduras first to see if it will work!"

He merely stated that Honduras would be the first nation in the world where the gospel would be preached to every creature!

As simple as that!

We have to obey!

We yearn to obey!

We want to obey!

It's as simple as that!

Once upon a time an angel spoke to a young lady, a virgin, and told her that she would be the mother of the Son of God.

That was really impossible, but not for God, and Mary did the impossible by believing God, and doing what He said to do.

"Mary said, 'I am the Lord's servant, and I am

willing to do whatever he wants. May everything you said come true'" (Luke 1:38 TLB).

What was Mary's secret of faith?

She heard God and did what He told her to do.

She, too, must have been "dumb" enough to do what God said to do!

Can we, the ministers and workers in the kingdom of God today, have faith enough to hear God, and be willing to do whatever He wants?

As we have thought about the great challenge that has been placed before us, many thoughts have gone through our minds, some of which we have written in this book.

As we write these final pages, the time is running out in Honduras!

Before you read this book, the census will have been completed.

Are we afraid to publish this book before it actually takes place?

No, because God told us to do it, and when God speaks, you don't have to ask His blessing upon the job He has given you; all you have to do is to be obedient!

We know it's going to work!

"Surely the Lord God does nothing, Unless He reveals His secret to His servants the prophets" (Amos 3:7).

"Behold, the former things have come to pass, And new things I declare; Before they spring forth I tell you of them" (Isa. 42:9).

That's what we're doing — we are merely sharing what God has spoken to us!

We were coming out of a restaurant in North Carolina where we had shared this vision with two pastors and their wives, and as we were saying, "Good night!" again God spoke and said, "Write that book tonight! Go back to your hotel room and dictate it right now while you are anointed!"

Would you believe we didn't have to "pray" about it?

We have heard many people tell us that God told them to do something and they said it was so big they had to "pray" about it!

Who do you pray to when God tells you to do something?

I have never been able to figure that one out!

We got back to the hotel room as fast as we could, grabbed our tape recorder and dictated until about one o'clock in the morning and finished the next day!

When God tells you to do something, do it, don't go back and say, "God, what did you mean?"

Recently a reporter asked President Bush a question.

He answered, "No!"

The reporter replied, "Would you explain what you mean when you say "no?"

President Bush said, "When I say 'no', I mean 'NO'!"

When Jesus said, "Go," He meant GO!

We appreciate the outstanding ministries that God has raised up in the world today!

We appreciate Marilyn Hickey and what she has done to get the body of Christ reading the Bible!

We love Larry Lea, one of God's most anointed servants, for hearing God's mandate to teach prayer! Because of his obedience to God, people are praying more today than ever in the history of the world!

We love Gary Whetstone, Dick Bernal, and many others who have taught us a lot about spiritual warfare!

We stand in awe of the ministries of Oral and Richard Roberts, Morris Cerullo, R.W. Schambach, Lester Sumrall with his mandate to feed the hungry, Jerry Falwell, John Osteen, Robert Schuller, Bill Bright, Billy Graham, T.L. and Daisy Osborn, Benson Idahosa, Reinhard Bonnke, Kenneth Copeland, Kenneth Hagin, and many others too numerous to mention, but we want to ask a challenging question!

What would happen if all of the ministries mentioned above would be willing to lay down their identities to pull together for a period of two weeks or even a month to fulfill the Great Commission to change a whole nation, how much could be accomplished?

As we have mentioned in other chapters, could all the TV ministries in America, all the denominations and all the evangelists cooperate to complete a simple task?

Can we all be so in love with God that we can see HIS plan instead of our own ministries?

The world will tell you that it is impossible, so we can only refer you to what God's Word says,

For with God nothing is ever impossible, and no word from God shall be without power or impossible of fulfillment (Luke 1:37 Amp.).

Once you have heard God, you can know that you know that you know that His Word is not without power, but meditate on the last four words, "OR IMPOSSIBLE OF FULFILLMENT!"

It will be done!

Soul Winner's Diary

NAME	DATE SAVED

Soul Winner's Diary

NAME	DATE SAVED

Soul Winner's Diary

NAME **DATE SAVED**

Soul Winner's Diary

NAME **DATE SAVED**

Soul Winner's Diary

NAME	DATE SAVED

Soul Winner's Diary

NAME **DATE SAVED**

Soul Winner's Diary

NAME **DATE SAVED**

Soul Winner's Diary

NAME	DATE SAVED

Soul Winner's Diary

NAME	DATE SAVED

Soul Winner's Diary

NAME	DATE SAVED

Soul Winner's Diary

NAME **DATE SAVED**

Soul Winner's Diary

NAME	DATE SAVED

Soul Winner's Diary

NAME **DATE SAVED**